Migration, Spawning Patterns and Conservation of *Hilsa* Shad (*Tenualosa ilisha*)
in Bangladesh and India

About the Authors

Dewan Ali Ahsan has been involved in field research and teaching at university level since 1999. He is interested in research focussed on fisheries and aquatic resource management, environmental management and risk management. He is involved in several national and international research projects. Dr Ahsan graduated from University of Dhaka and holds a European joint Master's degree and European PhD in "Water and Coastal Management" from University of Plymouth UK, University of Bergen, Norway, University of Algarve, Portugal and University of Cadiz, Spain. Currently, he is serving as a Professor and Chairman of Department of Fisheries at University of Dhaka, Bangladesh.

M Niamul Naser is Professor, Department of Fisheries, Soil, Water & Environment, University of Dhaka, Bangladesh. He has completed his Bachelor's and Master's major in Zoology from University of Dhaka. He was awarded the prestigious Canadian Commonwealth Scholarships in 1993 for PhD from the Dallhousie University, Nova Scotia, Canada. Dr Naser's extensive research skills enabled him to work with several projects inside and outside the country. Among them are *Adivasi* (plain & indigenous) cage culture with World Fish and BFRF; Urban Lake Pollution with BARC; Ecology of Cholera with University of Maryland, USA; Unprotected Coastal Sites of Bangladesh with Oxford University, UK.

Utpal Bhaumik, PhD from Kurukshetra University, Kurukshetra, India joined Agricultural Research Service of ICAR in 1976. He has served at the Central Inland Fisheries Research Institute, Barrackpore for more than 35 years in various capacities. He retired as the Head of Riverine Ecology and Fisheries Division of CIFRI. He actively participated in research on ecology and fisheries of rivers and estuaries of the country, especially *Hilsa* fisheries. He has about 200 publications in national and international journals. He was associated with different international collaborative projects of World Fish Centre, Malaysia; IUCN, India & Bangladesh, and WWF, India.

Sugata Hazra, Professor of Coastal Management, and Director, School of Oceanographic Studies, Jadavpur University, Kolkata, India, is involved in prediction and validation of Potential Fishing Zone in the northern Bay of Bengal, India, since 2007. He has done pioneer work relating to vulnerability and impact of climate change in Sundarbans situated in West Bengal, India. He is a member of the national task force for Bay of Bengal Large Marine Ecosystem (BoBLME) in India. Presently he is leading a project on ecosystem modeling, conservation and forecast of *Hilsa* fishery in the northern part of Bay of Bengal.

Subhra Bikash Bhattacharya, Gold medalist in Marine Science from University of Calcutta, started his research career in Marine Biology with special emphasis on fisheries, aquaculture and ecology. He obtained his doctoral degree in 2003 from Jadavpur University and standardised edible oyster farming technology in Sundarbans. Presently, he is working at Kakdwip Research Centre of CIBA and is dealing with various aspects of marine fisheries and sustainable aquaculture development in Sundarbans, India. He has contributed to a number of scientific publications.

Migration, Spawning Patterns and Conservation of *Hilsa* Shad (*Tenualosa ilisha*) in Bangladesh and India

Ecosystems for Life: A Bangladesh-India Initiative

Dewan Ali Ahsan
M Niamul Naser
Utpal Bhaumik
Sugata Hazra
Subhra Bikash Bhattacharya

ACADEMIC FOUNDATION
NEW DELHI
www.academicfoundation.com

First published in 2014
by

ACADEMIC FOUNDATION
4772-73 / 23 Bharat Ram Road, (23 Ansari Road),
Darya Ganj, New Delhi - 110 002 (India).
Phones : 23245001 / 02 / 03 / 04.
Fax : +91-11-23245005.
E-mail : books@academicfoundation.com
www.academicfoundation.com

in association with

IUCN

Disclaimer:
The findings/views/opinions expressed in this book are solely those of the authors and do not necessarily reflect the views of the publisher or the organisations they represent.

Migration, Spawning Patterns and Conservation of *Hilsa* Shad (*Tenualosa ilisha*) in Bangladesh and India

by Dewan Ali Ahsan, M Niamul Naser, Utpal Bhaumik, Sugata Hazra and Subhra Bikash Bhattacharya

ISBN 9789332701311

Typeset by Italics India, New Delhi.

Cover Photo: Ms. Sushmita Mandal

Printed and bound by The Book Mint, New Delhi.
www.thebookmint.in

Contents

Preface

Ecosystems for Life: a Bangladesh-India Initiative is a civil society led multi-stakeholder dialogue process to promote better understanding and improved management of natural resources in Bangladesh and India.

Bangladesh and India share some of the world's most intricate and complex river systems. The Ganges, Brahmaputra and Meghna Rivers, along with their tributaries, drain an area of about 1.75 million square kilometres and have direct impact on around 620 million people. These great rivers are inseparable from the history and legends of the region, as well as from the people who depend on them for their well-being. At the same time, the rivers face significant issues related to, biodiversity loss, navigability and flooding - issues exacerbated by the challenges inherent in managing trans-boundary ecosystems.

Ecosystems for Life was designed to help deal with these issues by facilitating multi-stakeholder dialogues among civil society actors. This encourages representatives of civil society, academia, the private sector and other organizations from both countries to engage in extensive dialogue and information sharing and, through research, produce timely and relevant recommendations for both policy and cooperative management.

Guided by a Project Advisory Committee comprising prominent professionals, legislators, diplomats and researchers from both Bangladesh and India, *Ecosystems for Life* has focused on five main themes: the links between food security and water productivity for poverty alleviation; the impacts of climate change, adaptation methods and mitigation strategies; convergence of inland navigation and integrated water resource management; the links between economic development and environmental security; and improving understanding of ecosystems and habitats, leading to improved conservation of flagship species.

The first phase of the project concentrated on analysis within each thematic area to identify significant issues, research gaps and priority areas for joint research. This analysis and consultation provided a clear agenda for joint research conducted through the formation of joint research teams (JRTs) consisting of researchers from both Bangladesh and India. Researchers used a common methodology for their analysis and developed a joint report.

This publication is an output of joint research conducted on the importance of migratory and spawning patterns for the conservation of the *Hilsa*, which falls under the *Ecosystems for Life* theme of improving understanding of ecosystems and habitats.

Hilsa is the national fish of Bangladesh and is also important culturally in West-Bengal, India. It is an important staple food and source of income for millions of people in the region. The focus of this research was prompted by recent serious declines in the *Hilsa* catch.

The objective of the research was to study migration and spawning patterns, methods of fishing, status of, and threats to, *Hilsa* in the region with a view to enhanced conservation. It also reviewed and assessed how current legislation and policy is affecting the species.

The research revealed a number of key issues including over exploitation, siltation in river beds, a decrease in water flow from upstream, fragmentation of the river in the dry season and a need to regularise conservation and protection mechanisms between Bangladesh and India.

After a series of multi-stakeholder consultations on the research findings a set of policy options and recommendations have been identified for policy makers in both countries. These include, among others the following:

- Ensuring ban on *Hilsa* fishing to protect the juvenile and brood fish should be imposed in both Bangladesh and India at the same time
- *Hilsa* migration depends on water flow and depth. To maintain proper

water flow, appropriate measures are needed at Padma-Meghna and Hooghly-Bhagirathi river systems.

- To ensure conservation of *Hilsa* and other fish species, a complete ban on use and manufacture of zero meshed nets is required.

- Establishment of any polluting industry and power station in the estuary or close to the spawning grounds is not advisable for the health of the estuarine fishery and mangrove ecosystems.

This joint research study highlights the urgency of adopting new measures to protect this important shared resource and the river systems, the *Hilsa*, depend on for their survival. It also clearly identifies the importance of working together across national boundaries to fully identify the complex issues affecting the health of a species like the *Hilsa*, and to adopt and enforce shared management regimes.

Acronyms

BFRI	Bangladesh Fisheries Research Institute
BWDB	Bangladesh Water Development Board
CCRF	Code of Conduct of Responsible Fisheries
CIFRI	Central Inland Fisheries Research Institute
CPUE	Catch per Unit Effort
CV	Correlation of Variance
DoF	Department of fisheries
DO	Dissolved Oxygen
DU	Dhaka University
FGD	Focus Group Discussion
GBM	Ganges Brahmaputra Meghna
GDP	Gross Domestic Product
GIS	Geographic Information System
GSI	Gonad-somatic Index
IUCN	International Union for Conservation of Nature
MCS	Monitoring Controlling and Surveillance
MINITAB	Statistical and Process Management Software for Six Sigma and Quality Improvement developed by the Pennsylvania State University
MPO	Master Plan Organisation
SAS	Statistical Analysis System is an integrated system of software
VGF	Vulnerable Group Feeding
LWR	Length-Weight Relationship

List of Tables and Figures

Tables

Figures

Background of this Study

Ecosystems for Life: A Bangladesh-India Initiative is an IUCN (International Union for Conservation of Nature) led multi-stakeholder research and dialogue process to promote insights into transboundary issues across three major river systems: Ganges, Brahmaputra and the Meghna. Research being one of the key components, the project has already undertaken six research studies in 2011 within the ambit of these themes and pertaining to the Bangladesh-India transboundary context. These studies were conducted by research institutions and experts from both countries working together as joint research teams (JRTs). The research topics were recommended from multi-stakeholder meetings arranged by the project. Under the biodiversity conservation thematic area the research topic was "The Importance of Migratory and Spawning Patterns for the Conservation of *Hilsa* in Bangladesh and India". This was carried out by a JRT comprising renowned researchers from both countries following an agreed common methodology that focused on the migration route of *Hilsa* with emphasis on the Ganges river system. The objective of the research was to study migration and spawning patterns, methods of fishing, present status of the fish in the region and threats to the species with a view to enhanced conservation. In particular, the study focused on following themes:

- Identification of migratory route and spawning patterns of *Hilsa*.
- Identification of types of human impacts affecting migratory and spawning patterns.
- Identification of approaches to ensure that migratory and spawning patterns are less affected by human activity.
- Reviewing and assessment of the extent to which current legislation and policy measures impact migration of *Hilsa* species.

Research revealed that the migratory route is well defined in Bangladesh, whereas, in India, the migration route has been traced only in course of the present study. *Hilsa* starts spawning migration upstream during the Southwest monsoon and its consequent flooding of all rivers. The spawning migration in direction of estuaries and rivers starts from July and ends in October in during the first phase and January until March in the second phase of events. Peak-breeding of *Hilsa* happens during full moon in October. The mean size of migratory population was around 750 grams to a maximum size of 1,500 grams.

Hilsa has a history of migrating to Allahabad and above in the Ganga river system from Bangladesh. Installation of a barrage in Farakka has completely intercepted the Hooghly-Bhagirathi migratory route of *Hilsa* from 1975 onwards. The enormity of *Hilsa* migration in Hooghly-Bhagirathi system was significantly low during 2011. Monsoon migration of *Hilsa* commences in July and gradually picks up momentum in August. From September onwards, the magnitude of migration is highly fluctuating and shows a downward trend. The mean size of migratory population was around 300 mm. In late monsoon, the mean size is reduced to 220 mm.

Over exploitation, siltation in river beds, decrease in water flow from upstream, fragmentation of river in dry season are identified as major human and physical effects on migration of *Hilsa*. The research team observed that the population is under strong pressure from fisheries. It is proposed that the species would benefit from more coordination between Bangladesh and Indian policy development and implementation of conservation strategies. A particular problem that requires urgent attention is the (illegal) use of extremely small mesh nets and the catch of juvenile *Hilsa* (*jatka*).

The Bangladesh Government has introduced an extensive *Hilsa* management action plan. The Government is trying to increase *Hilsa* production not only by conserving *jatka* but also by protecting brood *Hilsa* during breeding seasons by imposing a ban on fishing, restricted mesh size, etc. The Bangladesh Government also offers VGF (vulnerable group feeding) programmes for poor fishermen during the ban period. It is important to take follow-up action on the *Hilsa* report as recommended to introduce in West Bengal the steps similar to those taken in Bangladesh for *Hilsa* conservation. The present study suggests a replication of similar *Hilsa* Conservation and Management programmes in India. Uniform management policies of this transboundary ecosystem is envisioned to be a great way forward for maintaining sustainable ecosystem services in Bangladesh and India.

After a series of multi-stakeholder consultations on the research findings, a set of policy options has been identified that could be adopted in both the countries through advocacy to the involved policy makers. Accordingly, these were discussed in a policy meeting held in presence of relevant policy makers, civil society and resource users of both Bangladesh and India.

1

The *Hilsa* Shad

The Indian shad, *Tenualosa ilisha* (Hamilton), popularly known as *Hilsa*, belongs to the sub-family Alosinae of Family Clupeidae. *Hilsa ilisha* was rechristened *Tenualosa ilisha* by Fisher and Bianchi in 1984. However, the local name '*Hilsa* or *Ilish*' in use for over a century (Momi, 2007) has stood the test of time. The *Hilsa* has established itself as one of the most important commercial fishes of the Indo-Pacific region. It has a wide range of distribution and occurs in marine, estuarine and riverine environments. The fish is found in the Persian Gulf, Red Sea, Arabian Sea, Bay of Bengal, Vietnam Sea and China Sea. The riverine habitat covers the Satil Arab and the Tigris and Euphrates of Iran and Iraq, the Indus and Pakistan, the Irrawaddy in Myanmar, the rivers of eastern and western India *viz.*, the Ganga, Bhagirathi, Hooghly, Rupnarayan, Brahmaputra, Godavari, Narmada, Tapti and the Padma, Jamuna, Meghna, Karnafuly and other coastal rivers of Bangladesh. In fact, the *Hilsa* fishery in India and Bangladesh is dependent on the single species *viz.*, *Tenualosa ilisha* belonging to the habitats of Indo-Gangetic and Brahmaputra river basins (Figure 1.1). Though *Hilsa* is distributed to wide-ranging geographical area, it is mostly abounded in Bangladesh, India and Myanmar. At present, 50-60 per cent of global *Hilsa* catch is reported from Bangladesh, 20-25 per cent from Myanmar, 15-20 per cent from India and 5-10 per cent from other countries (e.g., Iraq, Kuwait, Malaysia, Thailand and Pakistan). The average *Hilsa* production of Bangladesh is about 3.5 lakh metric tonne/year. On the other hand, the production of Myanmar and India are 1.0-1.25 lakh metric tonne/year and 0.50-0.60 lakh metric tonne/year respectively. In the world as a whole, the average production is about 4.0-5.0 lakh tonne (DoF, 2008).

Hilsa (*Tenualosa ilisha*) is the most important fish species that links not only the transboundary ecosystems of India and Bangladesh, but also the life and culture of two neighbouring countries. During the period of undivided Bengal (until 1947), bulk of fish produced by the then East Bengal (now Bangladesh), used to be shipped to Kolkata fish markets (Ali, 1991) and markets of West Bengal and Assam in India.

The river Ganga is the most imperative river system in India and one of the largest in the world. The river system covers upland stream-warm water, swampy and deltic habits during its run from upper Himalayas to the Bay of Bengal. Many tributaries join the Ganga *en route* to the plain. The Yamuna is the most important arm and meets the Ganga on its right bank at Allahabad. From Allahabad, the river flows eastwards and on entering the state of West Bengal, river water is regulated through a barrage in Farakka. The main channel following Farakka Barrage flows South Eastwards all the way through Bangladesh acquiring the name of Padma, where it meets the Brahmaputra river, finally leading to the Bay of Bengal (Figure 1.1). A 41 kilometers long man-made feeder canal originates from upstream of the barrage and meets the Bhagirathi river at Jangipur in the South. Subsequently, the Bhagirathi flows for about 150 kilometers, thereafter joining Hooghly estuary in Nabadwip. The Hooghly flows through Kolkata finally leading to the Bay of Bengal.

Hilsa is into breeding migration in three major river systems of the Indo-Gangetic and Brahmaputra river network *viz.*, Ganga, Brahmaputra and Meghna. The species is all the rage in Bengali cuisine and highly prised in West Bengal, India, because of its distinctive taste and flavour. In India, presently, the fishery reserve of the species largely lies with the Hooghly-Bhagirathi—the component of Ganga river system besides other river-estuarine resources. The Ganga river system is listed as one of the top 10 rivers at peril by the World Wildlife Fund because of multifarious anthropogenic strain mostly pertaining to serious water withdrawal and indiscriminate pollution.

The flag-ship species of *Hilsa* in Bangladesh alone contributes to 10.82 per cent of the total fish production of Bangladesh to the effect of 2.89 million tonnes in 2009-10 (DoF, 2011). *Hilsa* soared gross domestic product (GDP) at a rate of 1.5 per cent. About 2-2.5 million people are either directly or indirectly dependent on it. Besides being a 'prise catch', ancillary involvements like transportation, processing, export, manufacturing boats and nets are fishermens' bread and butter. Therefore, economic contribution from this single species of fish is very high, in an agro-based country like Bangladesh. The average annual income of fishers shows high dependency on *Hilsa* fishing. Considering average *Hilsa* production of Bangladesh is

Figure 1.1

Freshwater Habitats of *Hilsa* in Indo-Gangetic and Bramhaputra River System

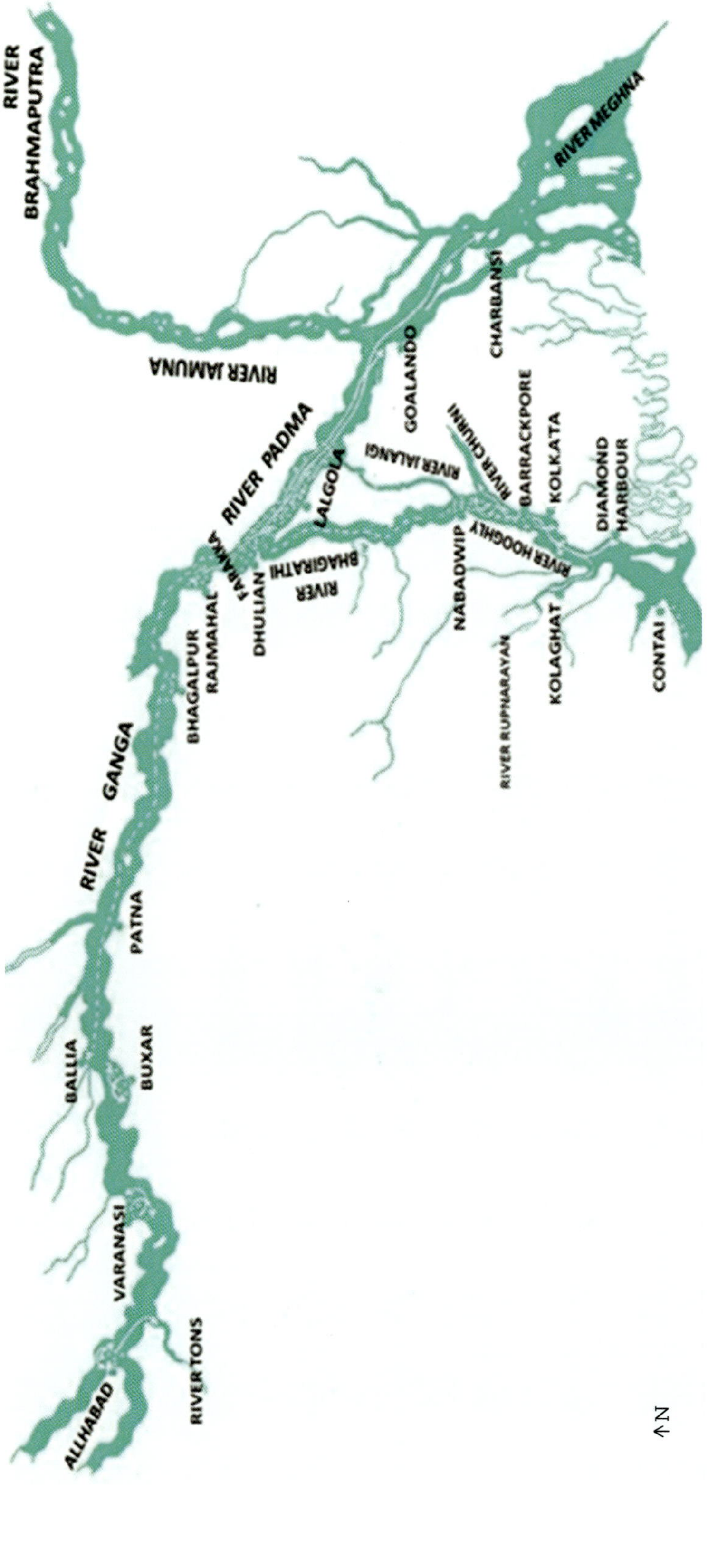

Figure 1.2a

Total *Hilsa* Catch of Bangladesh Inland and Marine Water During 2000-01 to 2010-11

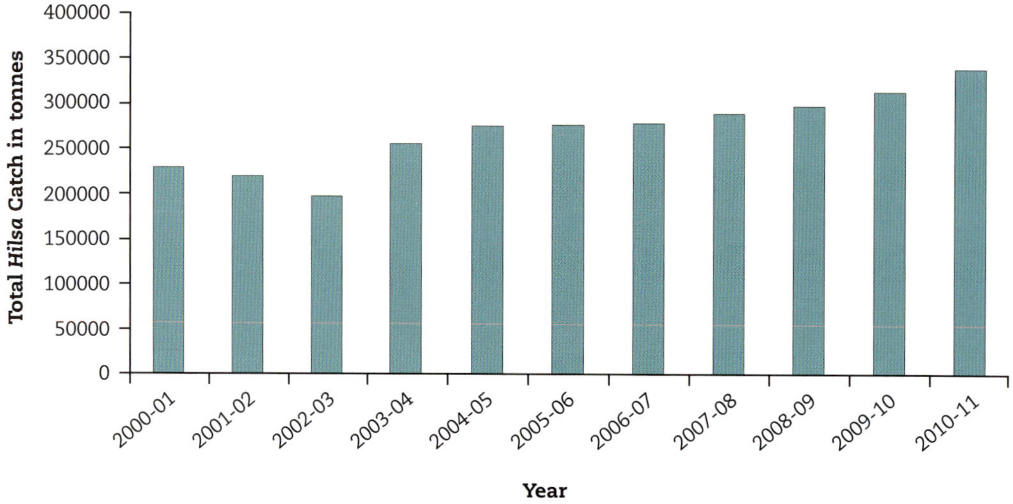

Figure 1.2b

Total *Hilsa* Catch of Hooghly-Bhagirathi River System During 2000-01 to 2010-11

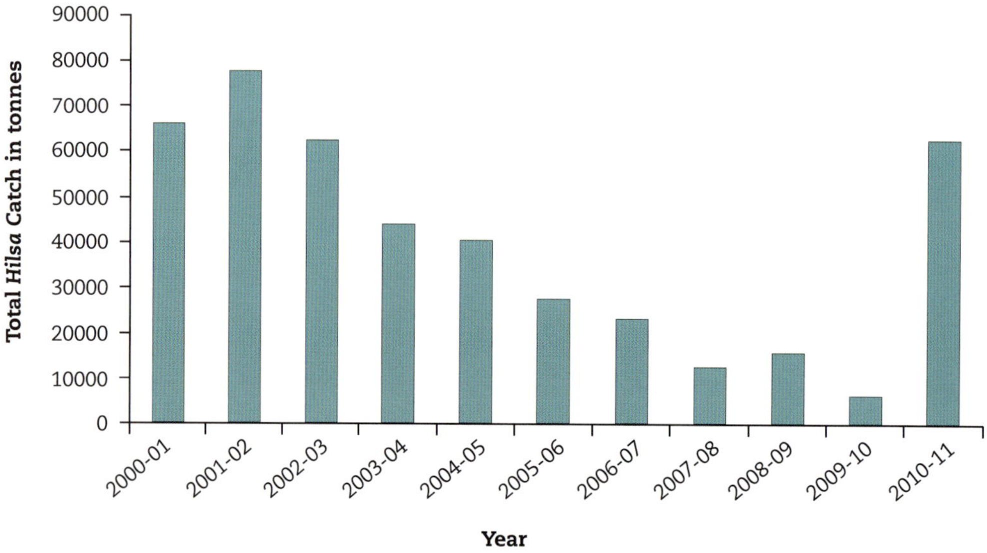

215 thousand mt (Figure 1.2a) to the tune of 380 million US dollars, contribution to gross domestic product (GDP) is 1 per cent. On the other hand, the Government earned an average 630 million US dollars by exporting nearly 220 mt of *Hilsa* in a year. Estimation says that 0.46 million people are engaged in *Hilsa* and *jatka* fishing. About 2 per cent of the country's total population is involved in the *Hilsa* fishery either directly or indirectly for their living (Bhaumik, 2011a). Summing up, *Hilsa* production helps alleviation of poverty in Bangladesh by absorbing her people in significant numbers.

Hilsa is also the major component of fishery in Hooghly-Bhagirathi river system accounting for about 20-25 per cent of total fish landing. The annual catch of *Hilsa* from the Hooghly-Bhagirathi river system has become highly variable over the years (Figure 1.2b). During pre-Farakka barrage period (1957-1974), the annual landing of this species varied between 114 and 6,573 tonnes with an average of 1,427.6 tonnes. Increased level of yield was observed after the construction of the barrage. The average annual harvest of *Hilsa* was recorded as 2,471 tonnes and 6,370 tonnes during 1975-76 to 1990-91 and 1991-92 to 1998-99 respectively (*Annual Reports*, CIFRI). *Hilsa* landings in the Hooghly-Bhagirathi river system during 2000-01 to 2010-11 varied between 12,733 and 77,912 tonnes (Department of Fisheries, West Bengal). Surveillances on production indicates that tremendous increase in effort from the 1990s with stepping up of mechanisation to catch this higher congregation of *Hilsa* in the estuary mouth also contributed to this manifold increase of *Hilsa* landing. In general, 80-90 per cent of the *Hilsa* is captured during monsoon months (July to October). It is observed that *Hilsa* fishery exists with the mean fish length varying in the range of 300 mm to 500 mm during June to August, in the middle range of 300 mm to 480 mm during September to November and in the lower range of 285 mm to 430 mm during January to March (Bhaumik and Sharma, 2011).

1.1 Types of *Hilsa*

1.1.1 *Classification of Hilsa Fishes*

According to Rahman (2005), there are two species of *Hilsa* in the Bay of Bengal. The *Tenualosa ilisha* (Hamilton) is locally known as *Ilish* and *Hilsa* shad in English. The other *Tenualosa toli* (Valenciennes) is locally known as *Chandana* and Toli shad in English. Unlike *Tenualosa toli*, the *Tenualosa ilisha* is migratory in nature. The distinguishing characteristics of the two species are given in Table 1.1.

There are numerous fishing gears used in inland rivers and sea both in Bangladesh and India. Some gears are identified as illegal, which indiscriminately kill juvenile *Hilsa* (i.e., *jatka*) due to small mesh size (Momi, 2007). In addition, gradual growth of industries in the upstream, urban growth, heavy duty use of fertilisers, agrochemicals and discharge of municipal waste to river system are polluting the river both in Bangladesh and India. Furthermore, climate change and its impacts in the Bay of Bengal may have had an inevitable impact to the

Table 1.1

Distinguishing Characters of Two *Hilsa* Species of the Bay of Bengal (Quddus and Shafi, 1983)

	Tenualosa ilisha (Hamilton, 1822)	*Tenualosa toli (Valenciennes, 1847)*
	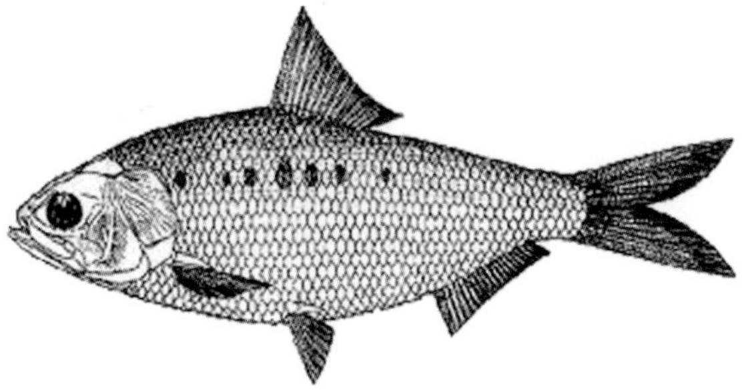 (Figure *Source*: FAO web)	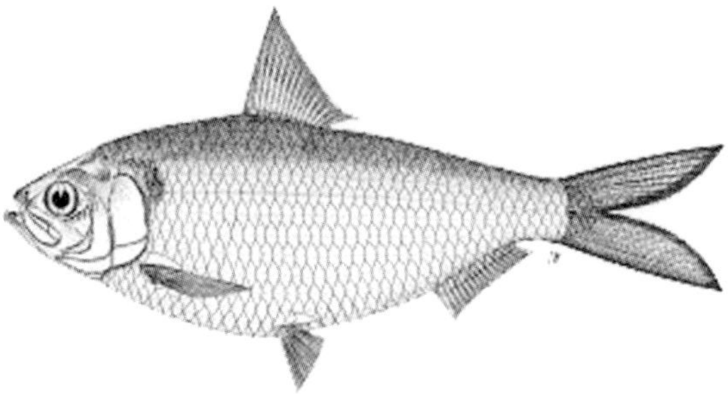 (Figure *Source*: FAO web)
Taxonomic formula	B.VI; D 17-19; P. 15; V.8; A. 20-23; C. 19-20; L.1. 46-48; L. tr. 15-19; G.R. 147-267/ 120- 200;	B. VI; D. 16-17; P.14-15; V.8 ; A. 18-20; C. 24; L.1. 39-41; L.tr. 13-15; G.R. 65- 103/ 70- 95;
Scutes	Prepelvic 17-18; postpelvic 12-14	Prepelvic 17; postpelvic 12-13
Median lateral scales	45-47	40-41
Caudal lobe	As long as head length	Longer than head length
Nature	Migratory	Non-migratory

Source: FAO web.

fish stock. Such multisided issues may have severe brunt on the endemic fish with immense wide spread collision in the near future to the stock. Only, timely taken proper management measures implementation will save the fishery and conserve *Hilsa* stock of the region.

1.2 Scope of Study

In view of understanding the impacts of anthropogenic activities on priced *Hilsa*, the International Union for Conservation of Nature (IUCN) proposed to establish a joint research team (JRT) comprising of experts' groups from Bangladesh and India. In the initial stage, a pilot project was taken up for identifying constraints and developing management norms to ensure migration and spawning of the species. The study was focused on the species' migration route in the Ganges-Padma/Meghna-Barak river system. Preliminary surveys revealed that few fish migrate through the Meghna-Barak river system leading to a focus on the Ganges-Padma System.

Specific objectives of study were:

- Identification of the migratory route and spawning patterns of *Hilsa*.
- Identification of the types of human impacts affecting the migratory and spawning patterns.
- Identification of approaches to ensure migratory and spawning patterns are less affected by human activities.
- Reviewing and assessing the extent to which current legislation and policy measures impact the migration of *Hilsa* species.

2

Methodologies

2.1 Study Area

For this study, 5 stations in Bangladesh (Figure 2.1a) and 23 stations in West Bengal, India (Figure 2.1b), were identified for monitoring by the research team. Bangladesh sites were predefined from previous works of Bhaumik (2011b), while Indian sites were chosen by the Central Inland Fisheries Research Institute (CIFRI) and the School of Oceanographic Studies, Jadavpur University, India. In Hooghly-Bhagirathi river system, selected sampling sites were located between 24°27.253'N, 87°54.47'E, and 21°34.834'N, 88014.223' E. The study was conducted all along the stretch of 523.59 km of the river, Bagirathi-Hooghly, Farakka, Lalbagh, Nabadwip, Kalna, Balagarh, Tribeni, Hooghly Ghat, Nawabganj, Baranagar, Bally Nimtala ghat, Godakhali, Raichawk, Diamond Harbour, Nischintapur, Harwood point and Frezergunj were situated dotting the stretch that came under research.

Figure 2.1a

Sampling Stations in Bangladesh

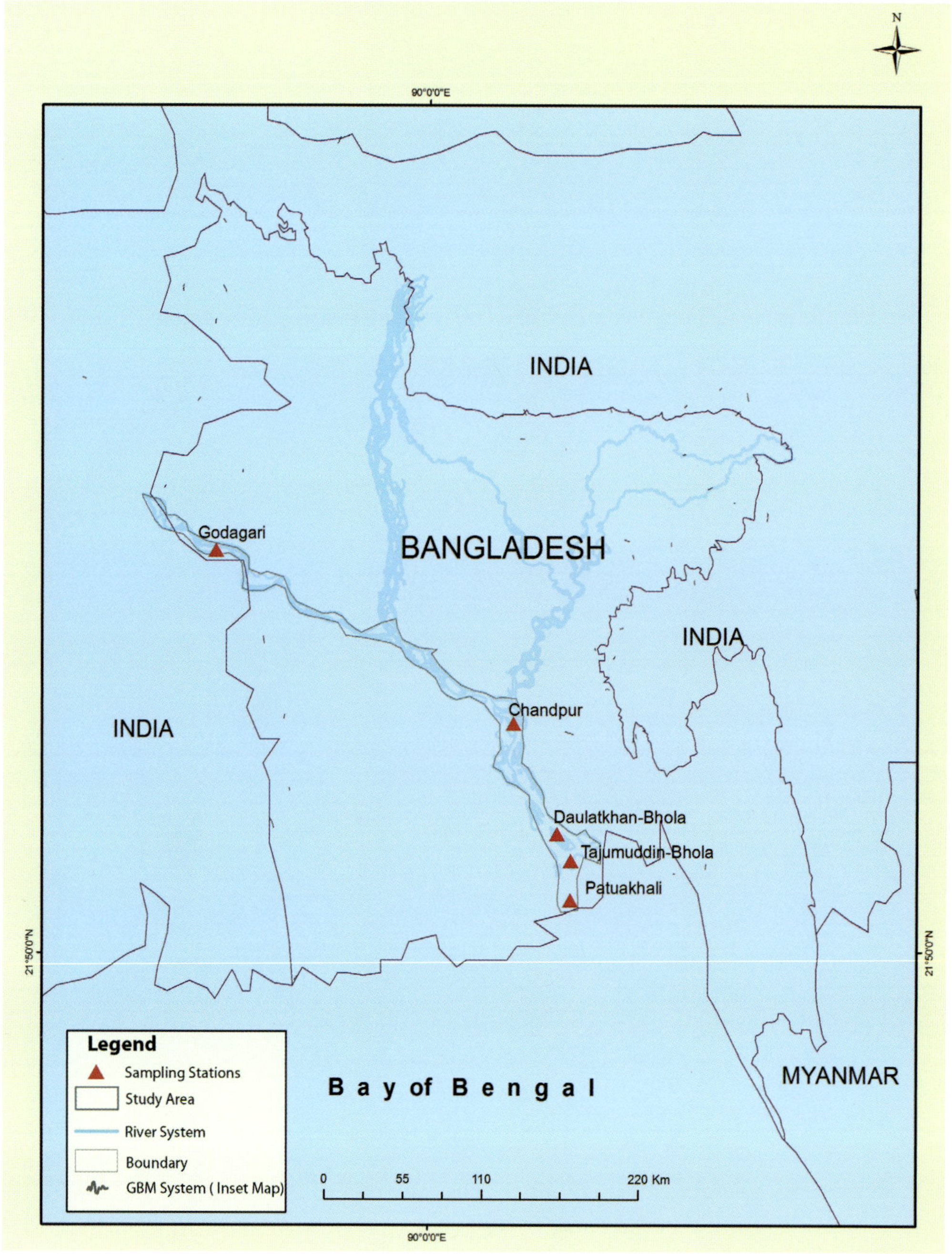

Figure 2.1b

Sampling Stations in Hooghly-Bhagirathi Stretch

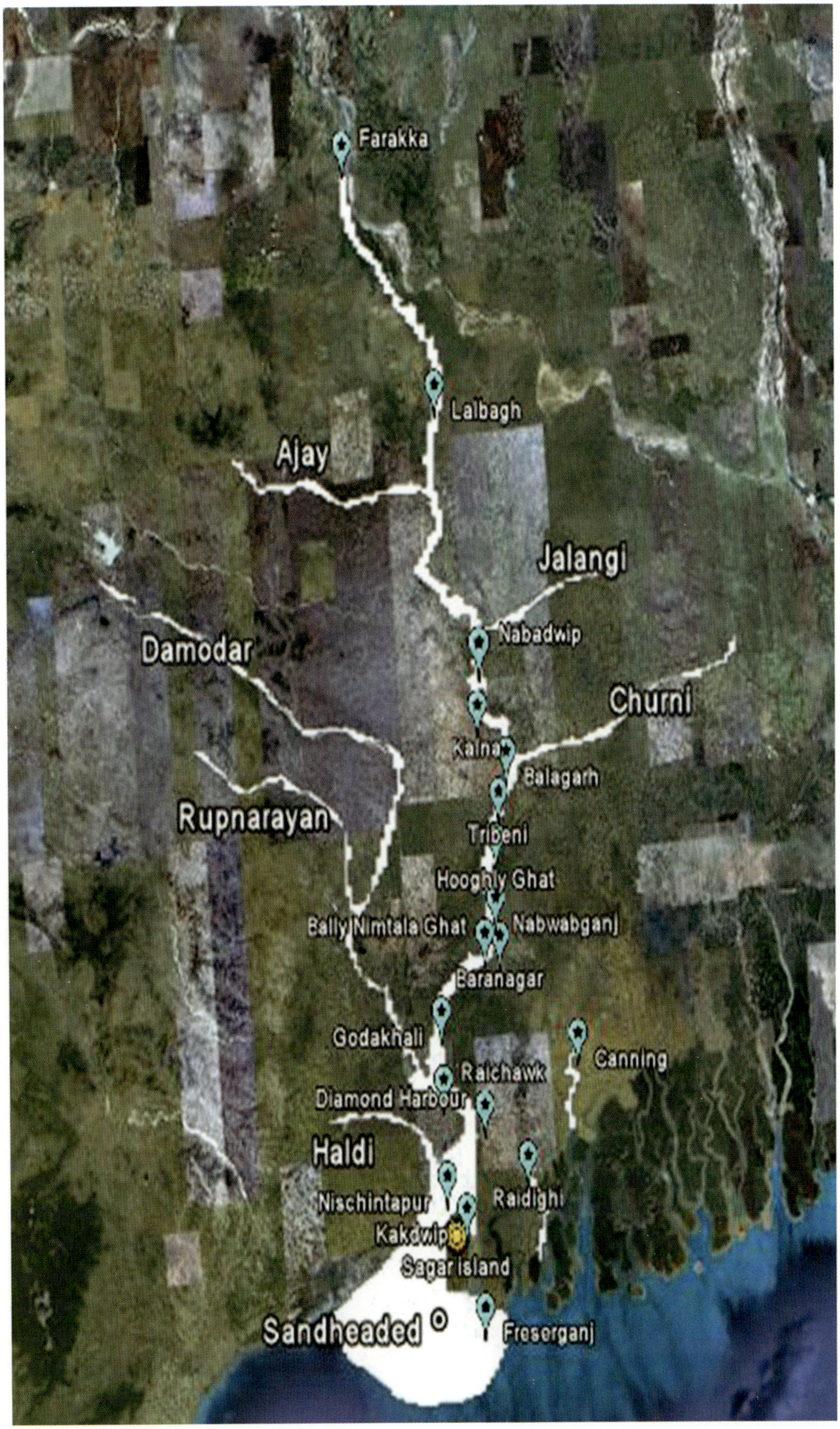

2.2 Materials and Methods

2.2.1 Method Used to Infer Habitat Quality

Water quality parameters *viz.*, water temperature, pH, dissolved oxygen (DO), salinity and chlorophyll-concentration were monitored vide method outlined by Strickland and Parsons (1968).

The measurement of temperature, salinity and conductivity of water were carried out by conductivity meter (YSI 30). pH meter (EcoSence pH 100) was used to measure the pH of water. Transparency of the water was determined with the help of Secchi Disk Visibility. To determine DO of the water DO meter (YSI EcoSense® DO200) was used. Alkalinity, hardness and ammonia were measured by a test kit (HACH-FF 2).

2.2.2 Habitat Quality Mapping

Habitat quality mapping was one of the main tasks in the study. Therefore, eight crucial habitat parameters were analysed using geographic information system (GIS) tools. The methodological steps used to carry out this task are as follows:

- Converting all water samples data into GIS data format.
- Statistical visualisation of all the water samples.
- Running outlier analysis of water samples to remove possible error and inconsistencies.
- Generating grid maps based on each parameter i.e., pH, water temperature, hardness of the water quality using point interpolation method of GIS.
- Validation of each grid raster data with Global Positioning System (GPS) ground data.

2.2.3 Methods Used to Infer Spawning

2.2.3.a An Identification of Spawning Grounds in Bangladesh

In Bangladesh, spawning grounds of *Hilsa* were recognised by the existence of mature and running (oozing) males and females and by catching *Hilsa* larvae with tentative fishing methods [Bangladesh Fisheries Research Institute (BFRI), 2011].

Eight water quality maps were used to identify spawning ground of *Hilsa* fish in Bangladesh. Acceptable range or key

Photo 2.1

Examination of Habitat Water Quality

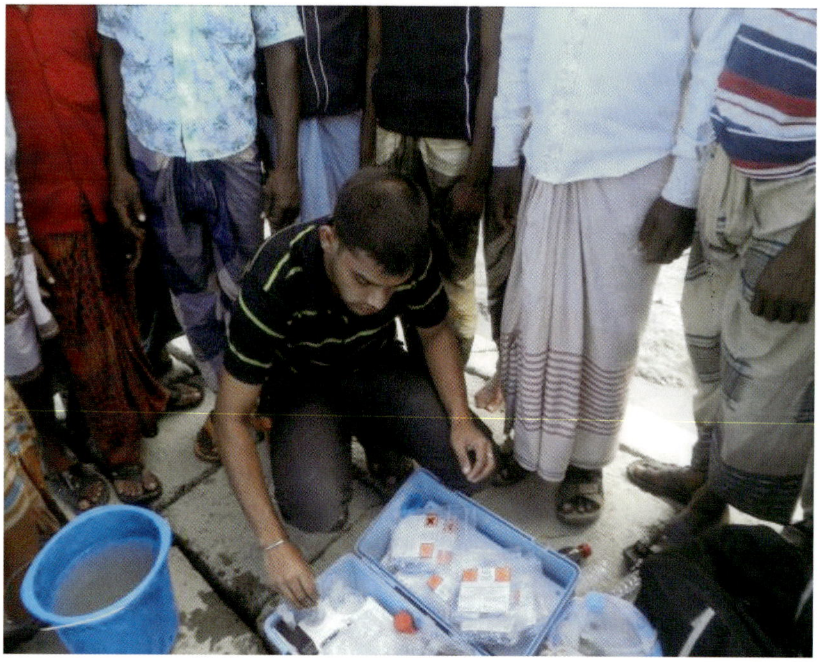

Table 2.1

Acceptable Water Quality Parameters for *Hilsa* Shad

Sl.	Water quality	Acceptable range	Rank
1	Hardness	66.30 Residual	1 0
2	pH	8.50 - 9.00 Residual	1 0
3	Transparency	13.33 Residual	1 0
4	Water temperature	30.15 Residual	1 0
5	Air temperature	29.12 Residual	1 0
6	Alkalinity	57.12 Residual	1 0
7	Ammonia	0.88 Residual	1 0
8	Conductivity	172.36 Residual	1 0

Figure 2.2

Weighted Overlay Modelling Using GIS for Identification of the Spawning Ground and Water Qualities of *Hilsa* Shad Migration Routes

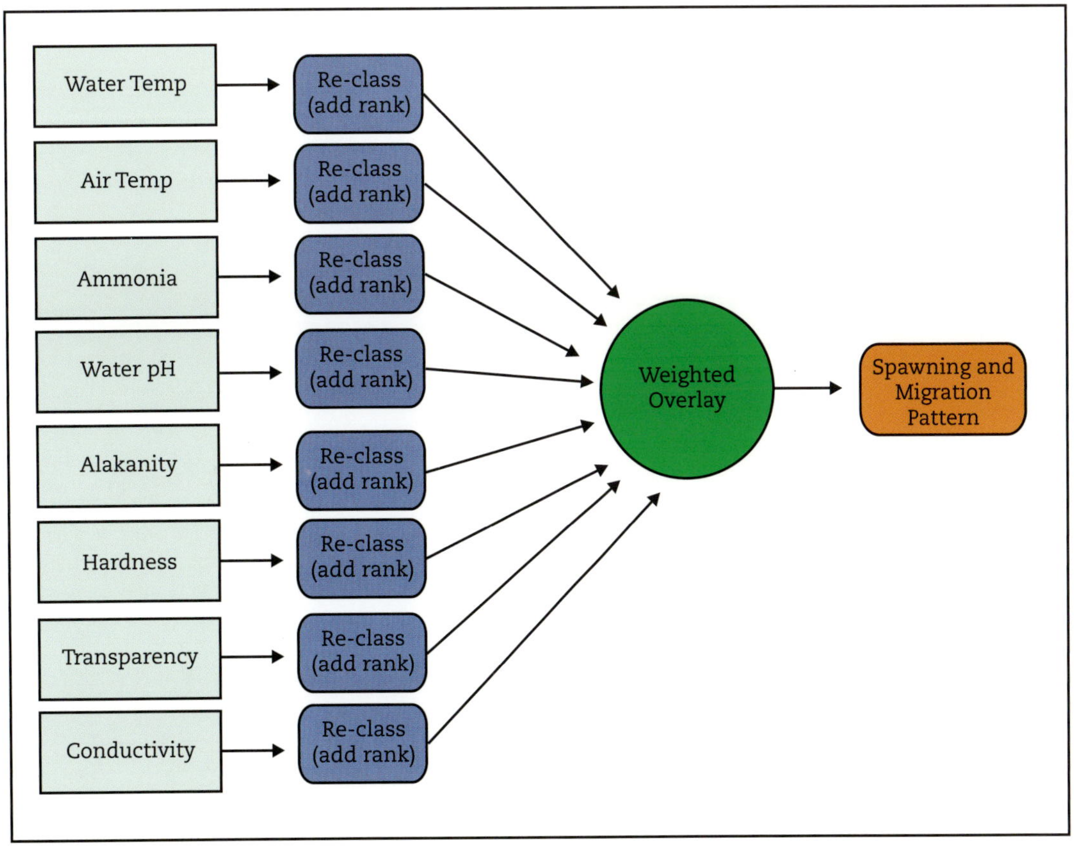

threshold of water quality for identifying spawning ground of the *Hilsa* fish was identified through a series of consultation meetings with experts thereby leading to workshops. On selection of parameters (Table 2.1), all key thresholds were converted in GIS thematic data format to run a weighted overlay model.

All acceptable ranges were tagged as suitable (1) and non-suitable (0) rank. This ranking was done to each habitat quality database using reclassification method. Ranked and re-classified data were added to a weighted model to identify the spawning ground (Figure 2.2).

2.2.3.b Identification of Spawning Grounds in India

In India, simple random sampling without replacement was deployed at each sampling centre for selection of fish samples. The data were collected from commercial catches. At various marine locations, hauls of maximum catch and their corresponding geographical locations were recorded using GPS to identify areas of aggregations of brood fishes. Net selectivity was ignored to obtain wide range of fish size. At each sampling centre, length (mm) and weight (g) was recorded with aid of meter scale and electronic digital balance. The data thus obtained from different sampling sites were pooled and analysed employing the software 'R' (R Development Core team, 2010). Juveniles were collected from bag nets operated in the system and catch per unit effort (CPUE) was calculated. Predictive seed availability map was drawn following Statistical Analysis System (SAS) 9.2 using contour plot *vis à vis* spline smoothing method.

GIS maps were prepared using data collected on various parameters from different sampling stations. Minimum curvature technique was used for surface modelling. The gonad-somatic index (GSI) was calculated according to Strum (1978) following GSI = weight of gonad (g)/weight of fish (g) × 100.

Fecundity of fishes was calculated through subsampling by gravimetric method followed by methodical count. The gonad weight of fish was measured before preservation in 5 per cent formalin. Preserved gonads were washed with simple water before counting. The eggs placed in petri-dish were separated and a subsample of 1 g of eggs was measured. The number of eggs in subsamples was counted. Five such sub samples were taken and mean value of eggs was used to extrapolate total number of eggs in gonads. More than 250 ovaries were used for the study of fecundity of *Hilsa*.

For studying maturity stages, the ovaries were first hardened in 5 per cent formalin and ova were examined at random from each ovary of fishes. For determining the stages of maturity of female *Hilsa*, estimation was made based on ocular microscopic study developed by Clark (1934).

Developmental stages were assessed as:

Stage I: Immature.

Stage II: Maturing.

Stage III: Maturing.

Stage IV: Advance stage of maturing.

Stage V: Mature.

Stage VI: Advance stage of maturity for spawning.

Stage VII: Spawning.

Data were analysed using MINITAB 16 and Microsoft Excel 2007 software. The length-weight relationship was examined employing conventional equation $W = aL^b$.

2.2.4.a Identifying Migration Route

In Bangladesh, migration routes were mapped on the basis of primary data collection like water quality and secondary data like catch along the riverside. Highest percentage (60%) was directly correlated with higher habitat quality with higher catch, whereas lowest percentage (1%) represented lower habitat quality and very low catch data. Since there are no fish movement data, both catch and habitat information were combined to identify the migration route.

In the marine and estuarine part in India, for identification of migratory route and biological analysis, fishes were collected from commercial catches with GPS locations of each haul in the estuary and sea. From the movement of locations of maximum aggregation of brood fishes, the probable migratory route has been inferred and used for preparation of maps in a GIS platform.

2.2.4.b GIS Analysis

For identification of the spawning pattern and migration route, all water samples were checked manually and statistically converted into separate grid file based on each parameter of water quality. Finally, various secondary data were combined with primary information for obtaining outcomes. The main methodological steps are given in Figure 2.3.

Figure 2.3

Methodology that was Adopted for GIS Study

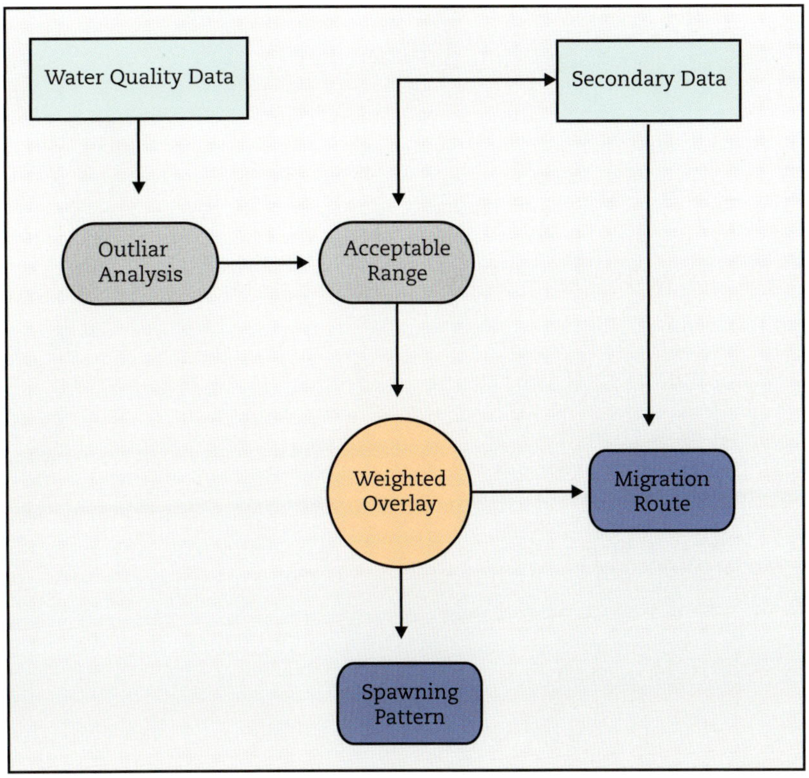

2.2.5 Socioeconomic Study

Fulfilling objectives required necessary data on fisheries. Socioeconomic aspects of fishermen were gathered through field observations. For this research, both qualitative and quantitative methods were deployed. Each approach served different but complementary roles.

Quantitative purists powerfully upheld that enquiries in social discipline should be objective, emotionally detached, and uninvolved with objects of study. Conversely, qualitative purists assert that multiple-constructed realities abound, and time-and-context-free generalisation of realities is neither desirable nor achievable. Qualitative research is more concerned with the what, how, why, where and when of things under query with a 'reflexive inquiry', whereas quantitative approach tends to be confined to amount or number of samples investigated.

Open-ended interviews were sought after in this study to gather information on issues of vulnerability, coping strategies, livelihood diversities, fisheries resources, gears, indigenous knowledge, conflicts, changes in fishing regulations, local institutions and other factors. Focus group discussion (FGD) was used and depending on information of FGD, a questionnaire was formulated.

For study on socioeconomic aspects in Bangladesh, 143 fishermen were interviewed, whereas in India 100 fishermen from both upper and lower stretches of Hooghly-Bhagirathi river system were interviewed through a structured schedule. Several group discussions were conducted in fishermen hubs with help from Fishermen's Associations.

2.2.6 Secondary Information

Secondary information was collected from available authentic sources of data. References are cited separately.

3

Understanding the *Hilsa* Fish Habitat Quality, Migration Patterns and Spawning Grounds

3.1 Habitat Quality in Padma River and Meghna Estuary of Bangladesh

3.1.1 Air and Water Temperature

The *in situ* air-temperature (Figure 3.1a) during spawning season showed maximum value in the upstream Rajshahi region, whereas minimum was noted in the coastal water area. Upper Meghna area of Chandpur shows moderate values.

Water temperature was lowest at the upstream Rajshahi area, whereas water temperature was highest in the Meghna river at Chandpur (Figure 3.1b). Water temperature was moderate in coastal area during the spawning period of 2011.

3.1.2 pH

The pH was lowest in upstream of the Padma river at Rajshahi. It gradually increased towards the coastal area. However, pH values were neutral in the Padma river system and gradually turned basic in Meghna river and coastal ecosystem. The pH shows the suitability of breeding ground throughout the river system (Figure 3.1c).

3.1.3 Alkalinity

The alkalinity was lowest in Chandpur Meghna river system whereas highest in Paba and Godagari in upstream Padma river system. However, in the spawning ground, the alkalinity was moderate. It is to be noted that higher alkalinity in the upstream may be due to Barind soil of the area (Figure 3.1d).

3.1.4 Hardness

Hardness was lowest in Chandpur and upper Meghna basins. The hardness was moderately higher in the lower Meghna estuary and highest in the Rajshahi region (Figure 3.1). End results corresponded to nature of alkanity of water and may have had similar reasons.

3.1.5 Transparency

Transparency of water showed that the river water was less turbid in Rajshahi and coastal area. However, it was highly turbid in Chandpur area, i.e., the upper Meghna area (Figure 3.1f). It is generally believed that *Hilsa* needs turbid water to migrate and may use less transparent water to breed. The Padma river water transparency was found to be suitable for breeding. However, other factors like water depth and flow may be considered for identification of breeding grounds.

3.1.6 Conductivity

The conductivity was lowest in Chandpur Meghna river system, while highest in upstream of river Padma and the lower in Meghna basin of coastal area. It is to be noted that moderate value was seen in Bhola spawning area during the sampling (Figure 3.1g). The conductivity corresponds with readings on transparency. Besides turbid water, agricultural waste may contribute to values of conductivity.

3.1.7 Ammonia

The ammonia level was lowest in the Padma river system at Rajshahi and highest in lower Meghna coastal water area. The Chandpur area was moderate in nature. The release of waste from Chandpur downwards to coastal area was high (Figure 3.1h). This may be caused due to agricultural lands or plant and animal remains in the river system.

3.2 Habitat Quality Mapping in Hooghly River System

3.2.1 Threshold Values of Physic-chemical Parameters for Hilsa Migration, Breeding and Rearing

Hilsa (*Tenualosa ilisha*) has year round fishery with two distinguished peaks of monsoon and winter in Bhagirathi-Hooghly linkage of Ganga river system. These peaks constitute brood stocks of *Hilsa* with varying maturity stages. The monsoon peak forms of 90–95 per cent matured *Hilsa*, while the winter stocks are mixed population of immature and mature fishes. Prolonged and extensive monitoring of migratory and breeding behaviour and rearing grounds of *Hilsa* enables us to identify some physico-chemical and biological factors which are collectively responsible for stimulation thus triggering migration of adult *Hilsa* into the system.

The monsoon runoff of hugely turbid water above 100 NTU (preferably 100–140 NTU) turbidity is prime requisite for attracting

Figure 3.1a

GIS Mapping for Water Quality (Air Temperature) for the Padma and Meghna River System During the Spawning Period of 2011

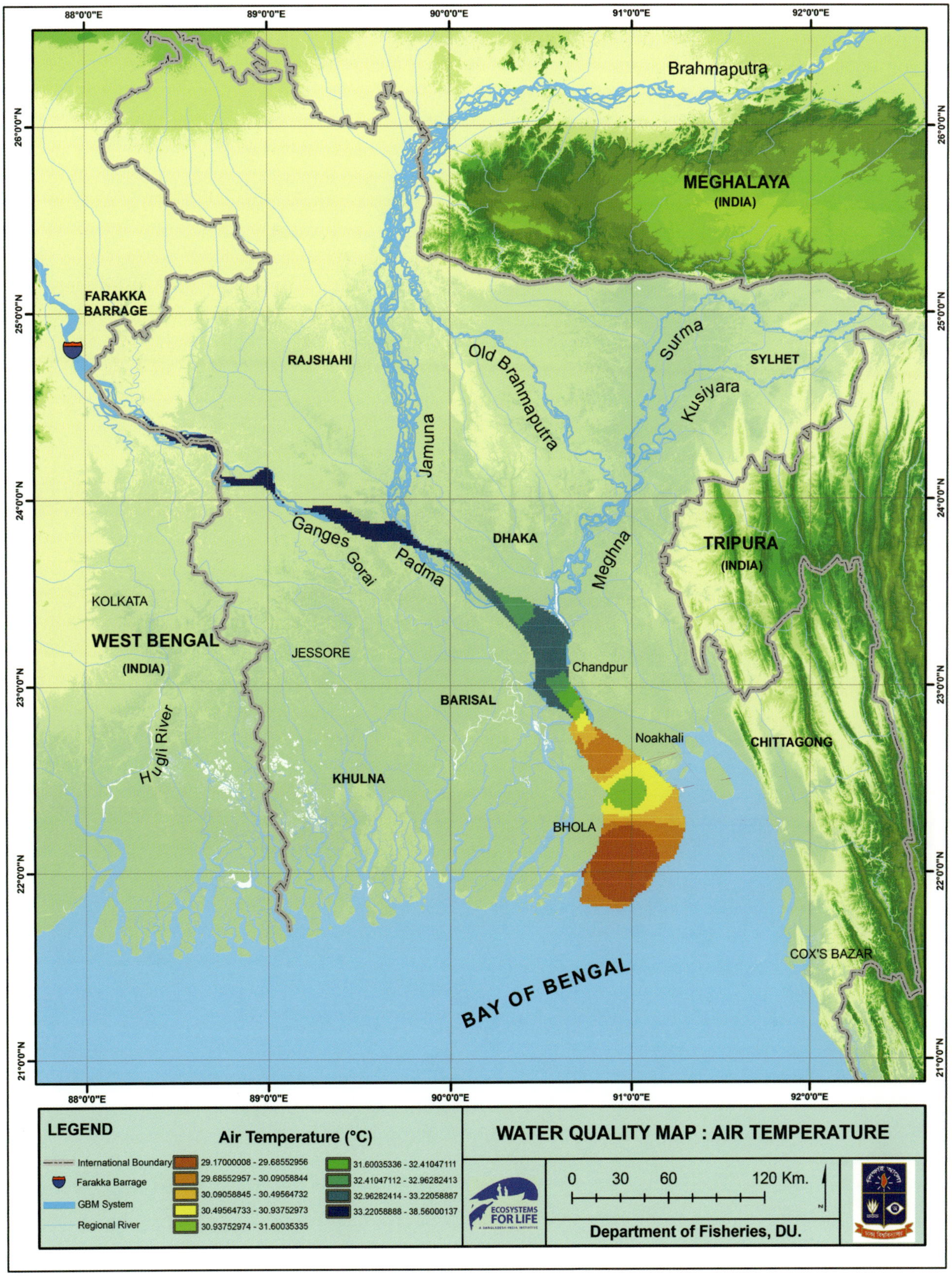

Figure 3.1b

GIS Mapping for Water Quality (Water Temperature) for the Padma and Meghna River System During the Spawning Period of 2011

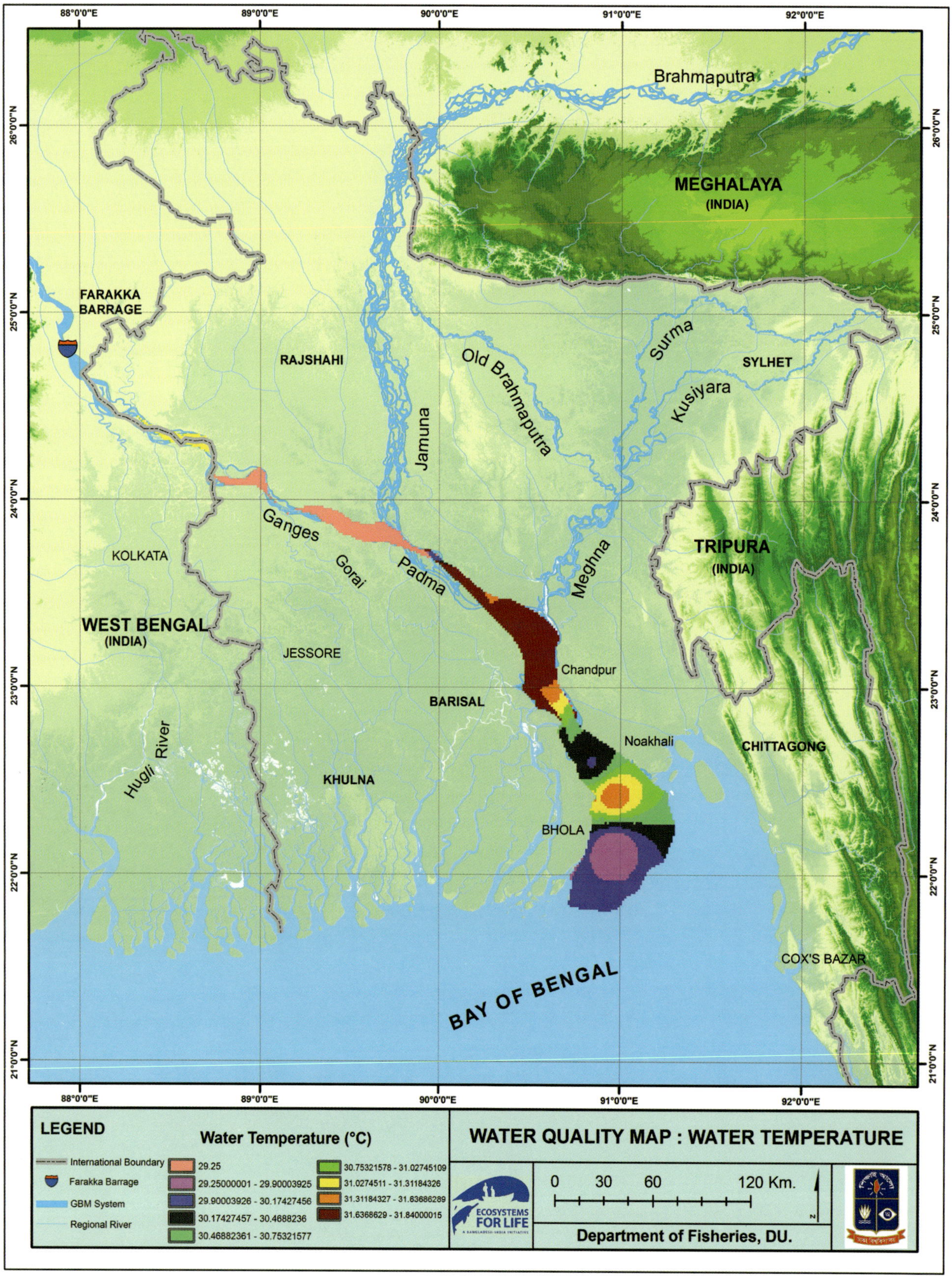

Figure 3.1c

GIS Mapping for Water Quality (pH) for the Padma and Meghna River System During the Spawning Period of 2011

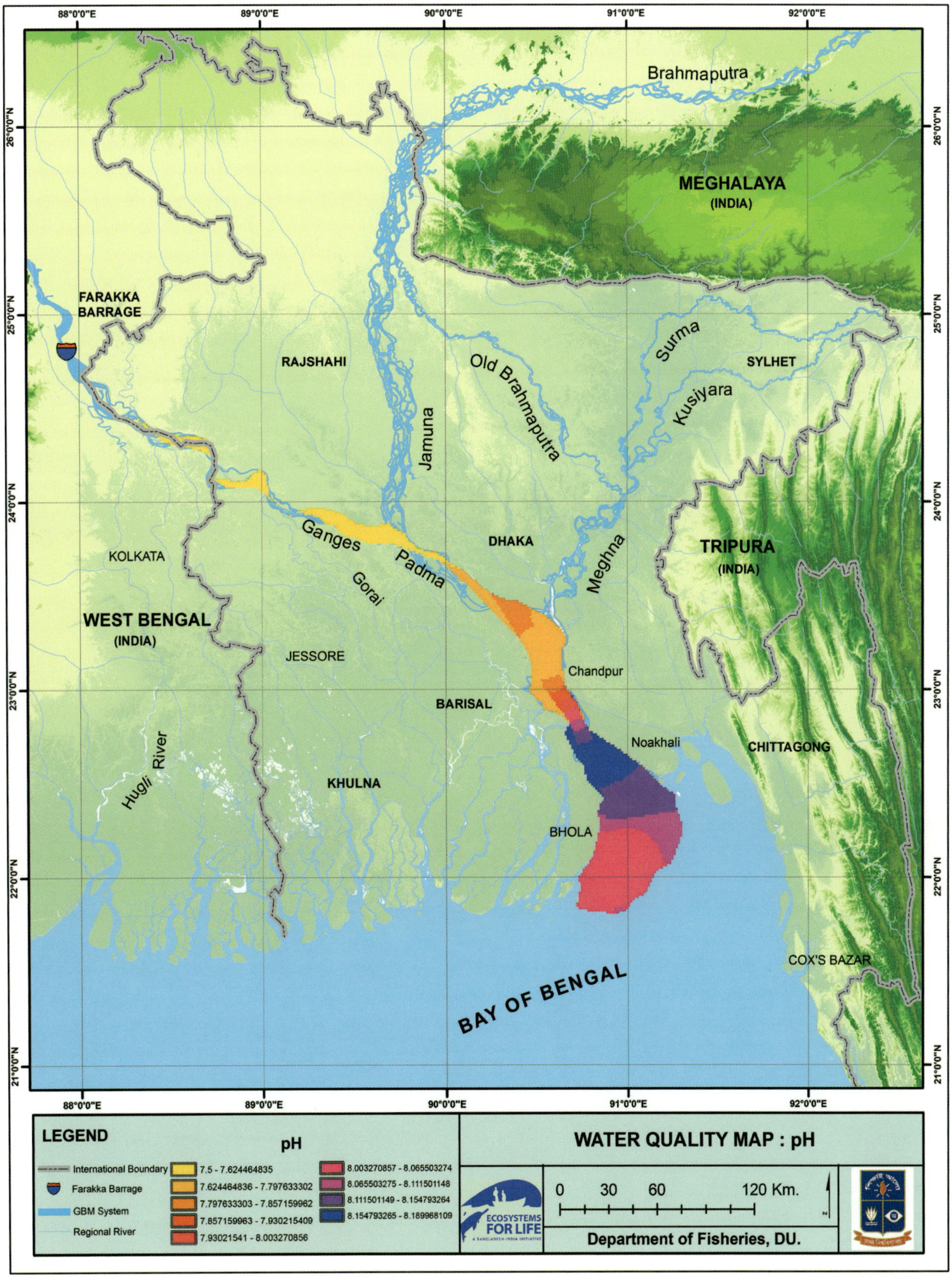

Figure 3.1d

GIS Mapping for Water Quality (Alkalinity) for the Padma and Meghna River System During the Spawning Period of 2011

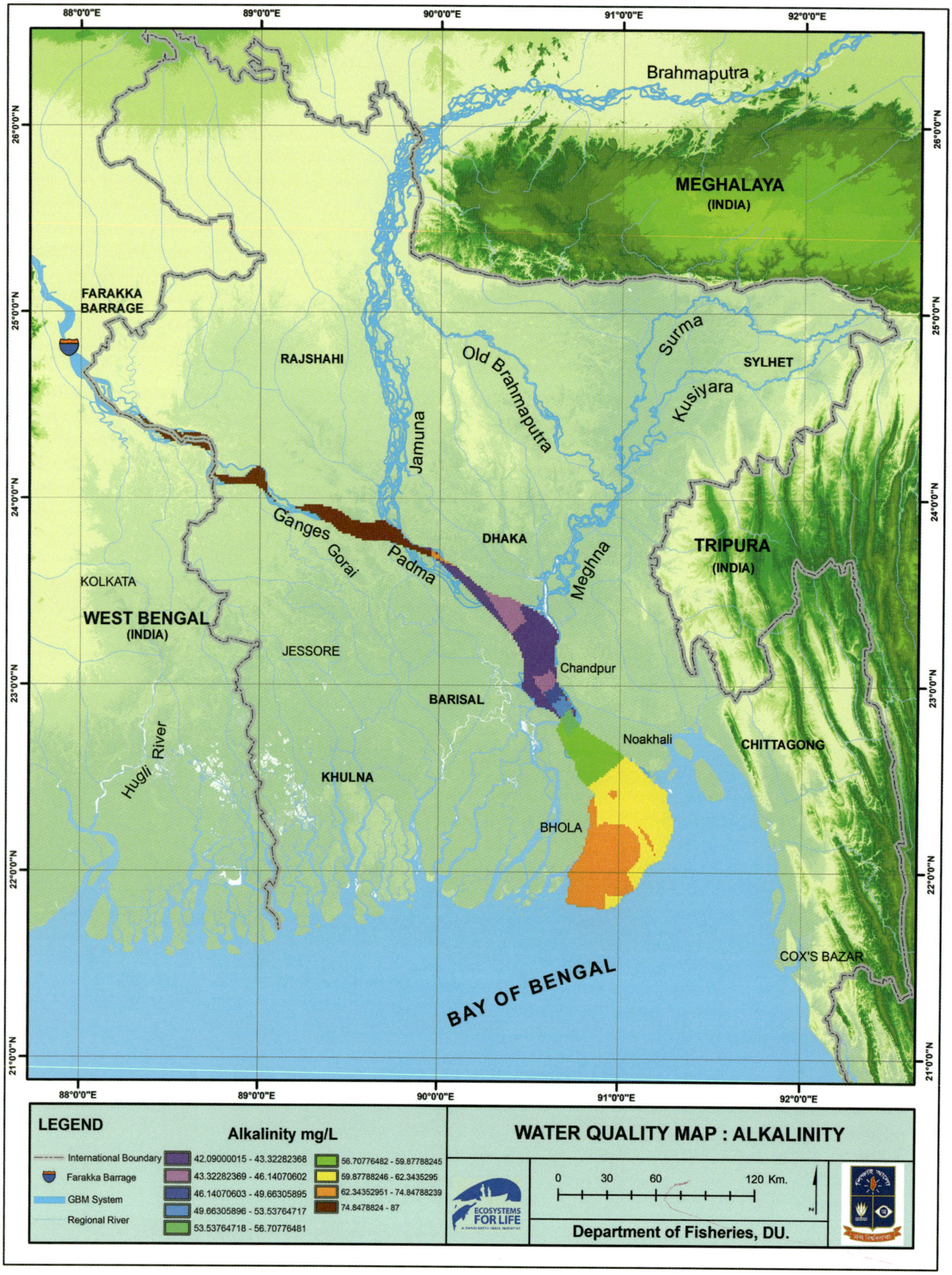

Figure 3.1e

GIS Mapping for Water Quality (Hardness) for the Padma and Meghna River System During the Spawning Period of 2011

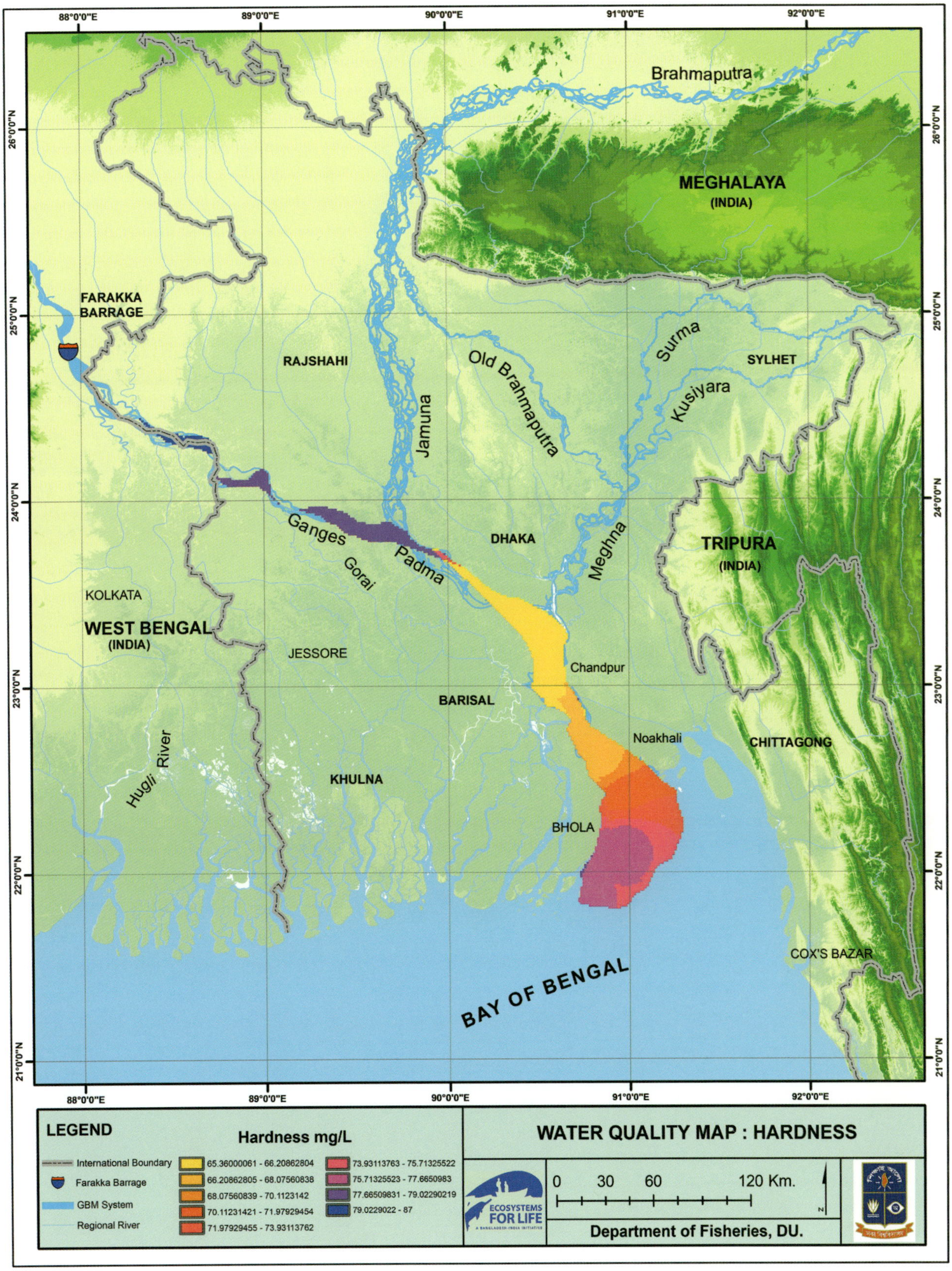

Figure 3.1f

GIS Mapping for Water Quality (Transparency) for the Padma and Meghna River System During the Spawning Period of 2011

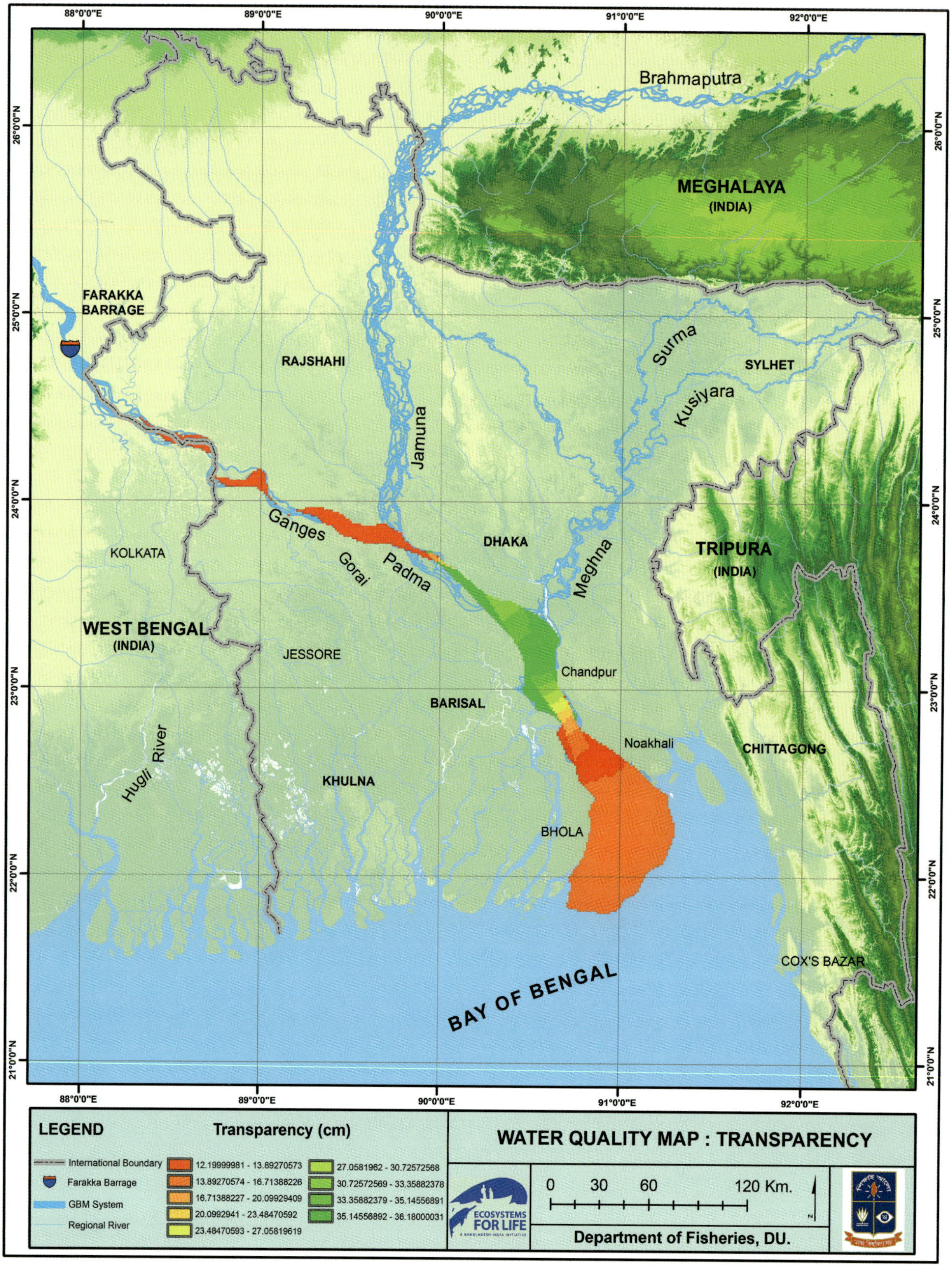

Figure 3.1g

GIS Mapping for Water Quality (Conductivity) for the Padma and Meghna River System During the Spawning Period of 2011

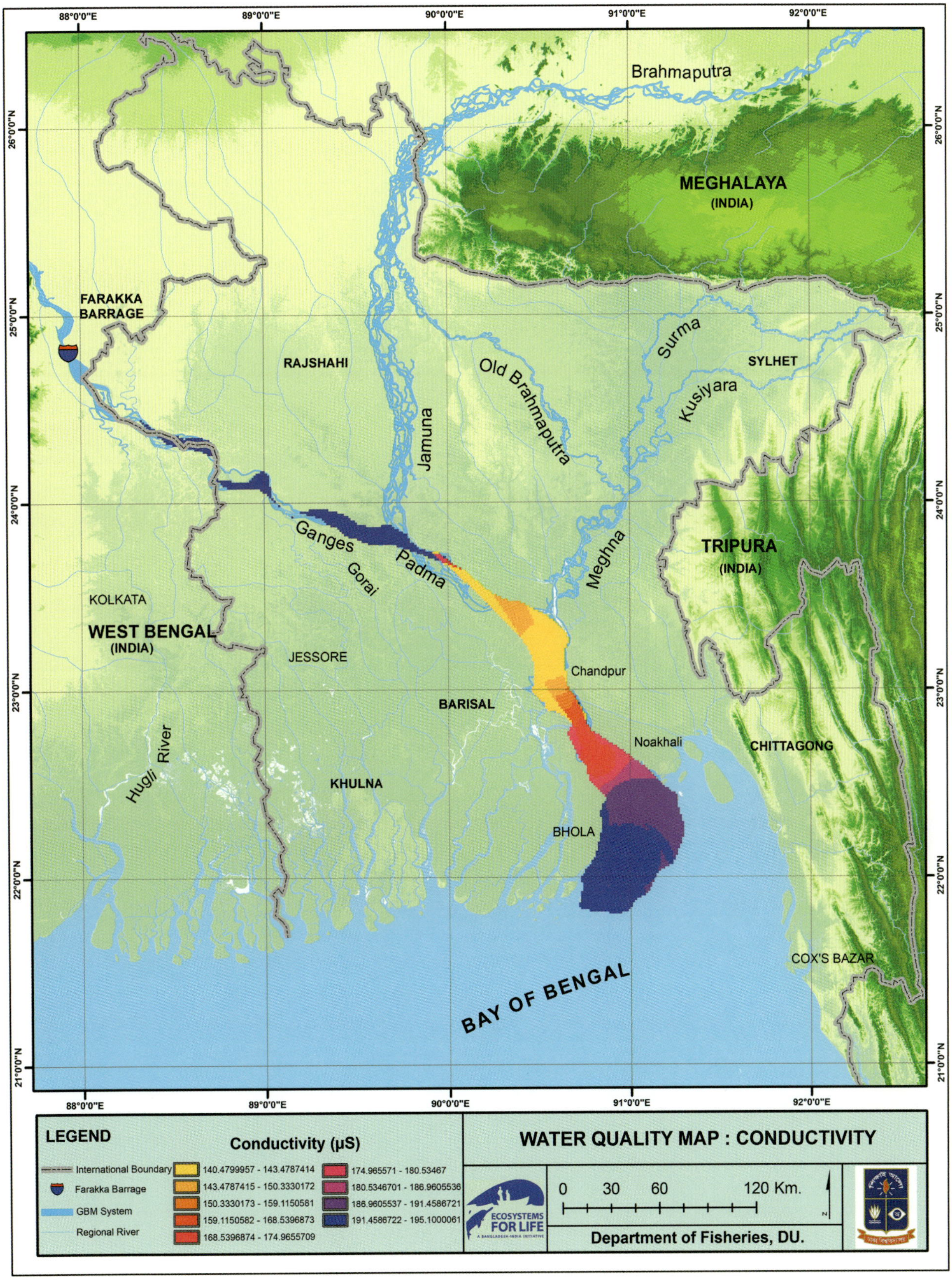

Figure 3.1h

GIS Mapping for Water Quality (Amonia) for the Padma and Meghna River System During the Spawning Period of 2011

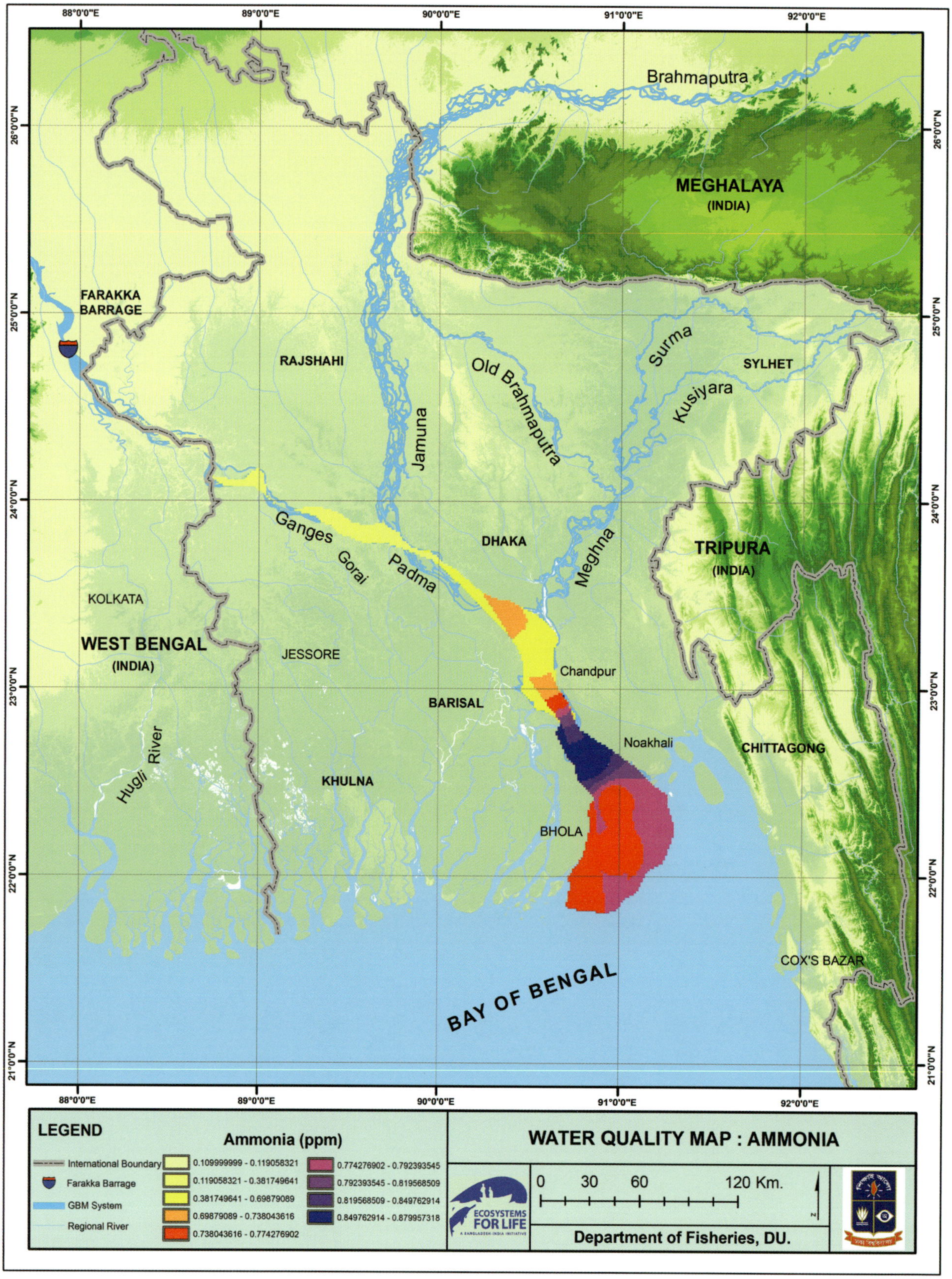

Table 3.1

Threshold Values of Physico-Chemical Parameters for *Hilsa* Migration, Breeding and Rearing in Bangladesh

	Breeding Activities	*Nursery Activities*
Depth	20 m and above for migration and pre-breeding congregation	Comparatively shallower depth near river-estuarine margins above the congregation grounds
Turbidity (NTU)	100-140	Comparatively low turbid areas (70-80 NTU)
Temperature (°C)	29.3-30.2	29.8-30.8
Salinity (ppt)	<0.1	<0.1
DO (ppm)	5.0-6.8	4.8-6.8
pH	7.70-8.30	7.9-8.40
Chlorophyll (µg/l)	0.114-0.180	0.140-0.180

shoals of brood *Hilsa* to the Hooghly-Bhagirathi system. Depth plays limited role in movement of migrating *Hilsa* and water column of 18-20 m has been observed to be ideal for stress free movement of brood stocks. Of course the *Hilsa* fishes pass through comparatively lower depth (av. 10 m) in winter months. It is worth mentioning here that the size of migratory *Hilsa* in the winter is smaller than that of the monsoon season. Temperature of river-estuarine water has been observed to drop by 1.5°C from average of 31.3°C (29.5-32.6°C) to 29.8°C (29.3-30.2°C) during monsoon migration of the brood fishes. On the other hand, in late winter (February) the ambient temperature rises by 1.8°C from an average of 27.6°C (26.8-28.4°C) to 28.6°C (27.0-31.8°C) which might influence upstream migration and breeding of *Hilsa*.

Among chemical factors, salinity plays a determining role in breeding migration of *Hilsa* into the system. Since salinity of the estuarine-river system remains below 0.1 ppt for greater part of the year, migration and resultant breeding activities of *Hilsa* never get hindered within the system. In the riverine system, fishes get alkaline environment (pH 7.7-8.3) during their stay and life span. Dissolved oxygen (DO) content of the system by and large fluctuates in the range of 5.0-7.0 ppm. However, during monsoon, the average oxygen increases by 1.22 ppm from 4.63 ppm to 5.85 ppm.

Chlorophyll values of the river-estuarine system fluctuated between 0.114 and 0.180 µg/l during monsoon period. It has been observed that values are comparatively more in some stretches where nursery grounds have been located.

While mentioning the threshold values of hydrography and physico-chemical parameters for breeding and nursery activities of *Hilsa*, the conditions given in Table 3.1 were recorded and considered ideal for the Hooghly-Bhagirathi river system.

3.2.2. Meteorological Observations

Perusal of Figures 3.2 and 3.3 reveals that month-wise average rainfall during 2010 was almost static between May and August (123.0-169.0 mm) with little rise in September (288.5 mm). Low rainfall and resultant shortfall in required depth and related hydro-ecological conditions affected breeding migration and population recruitment of *Hilsa* during 2011. Rainfall during 2011 was much higher with a rising trend from June onwards and attained peak during August (646.8 mm). The temperature was higher (24.24-34.31°C) during June to October in 2010 compared to 2011 (22.20-32.87°C) for the same period. The impact of inadequate rainfall and temperature variation on breeding failure in 2010 was reflected in the magnitude of migration *vis-à-vis* poor catch of *Hilsa* in the following year 2011.

3.2.3. Hydrographical Observations: Depth

Depth profile revealed unevenness of river-estuarine course, which varied with tidal amplitude and volume of river discharge. Depth was as high as 58-68 ft (17.67-20.42 m) between Hooghly Ghat and Kalna and 60 ft (18.28 m) around Lalbagh in July-August.

Figure 3.2

Variation in Temperature (Max-Min), Rainfall and Humidity in 2010

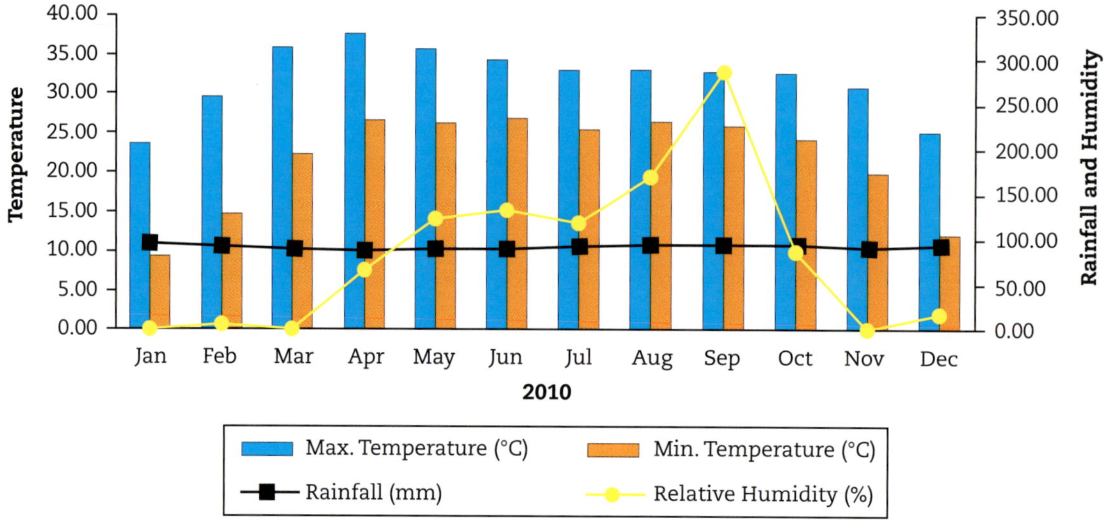

Figure 3.3

Variation in Temperature (Max-Min), Rainfall and Humidity During January-October, 2011

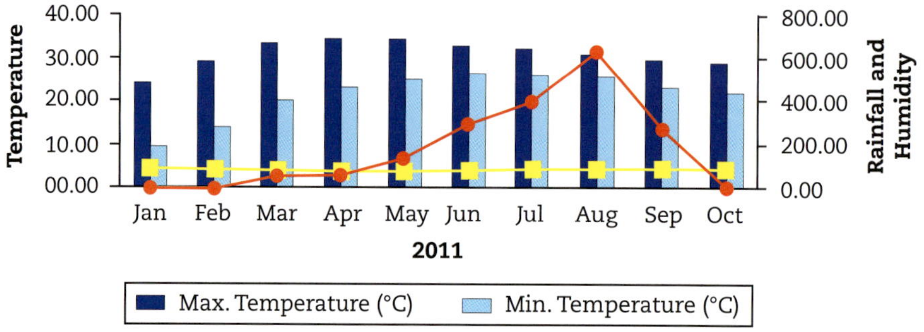

September onwards, the depth in upper reaches decreased whereas it increased in the lower zone below Diamond Harbour. The remaining part of the river-estuarine course was comparatively shallower with depth ranging between 38 ft (11.58 m) to 45 ft (13.71 m) in monsoon and further reduction in post-monsoon period.

3.2.4 Hydrological Investigations

Hydrological investigation included study of turbidity, water temperature, transparency, total suspended solids, DO, pH, salinity and chlorophyll *in situ*. Hydrological information is important since *Hilsa* needs favourable water conditions for its migration and spawning. (Figure 3.4a-e).

Figure 3.4a

Various Aspects of Hydrological Investigations (Water Temperature)

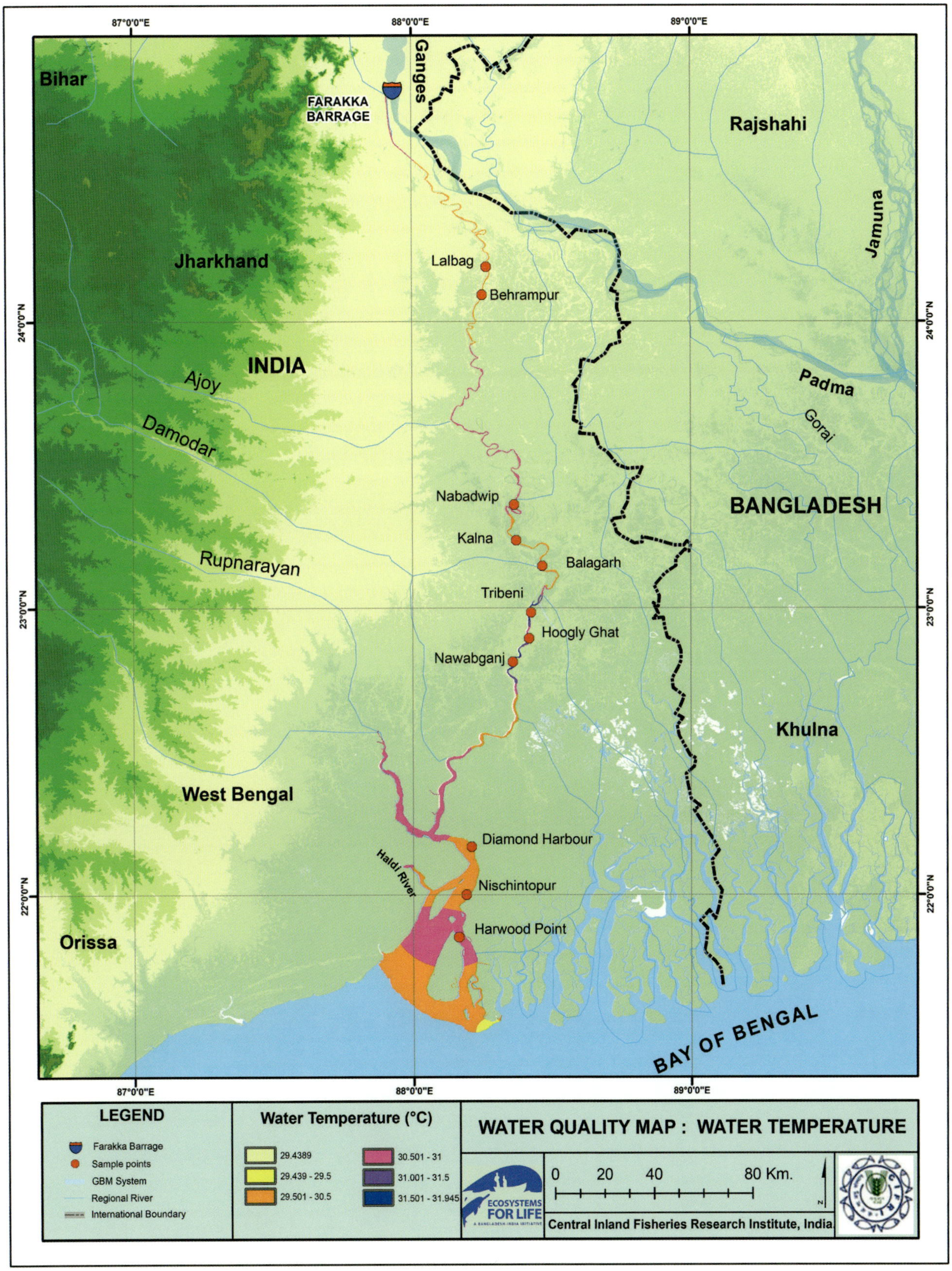

Figure 3.4b

Various Aspects of Hydrological Investigations (Water Transparency)

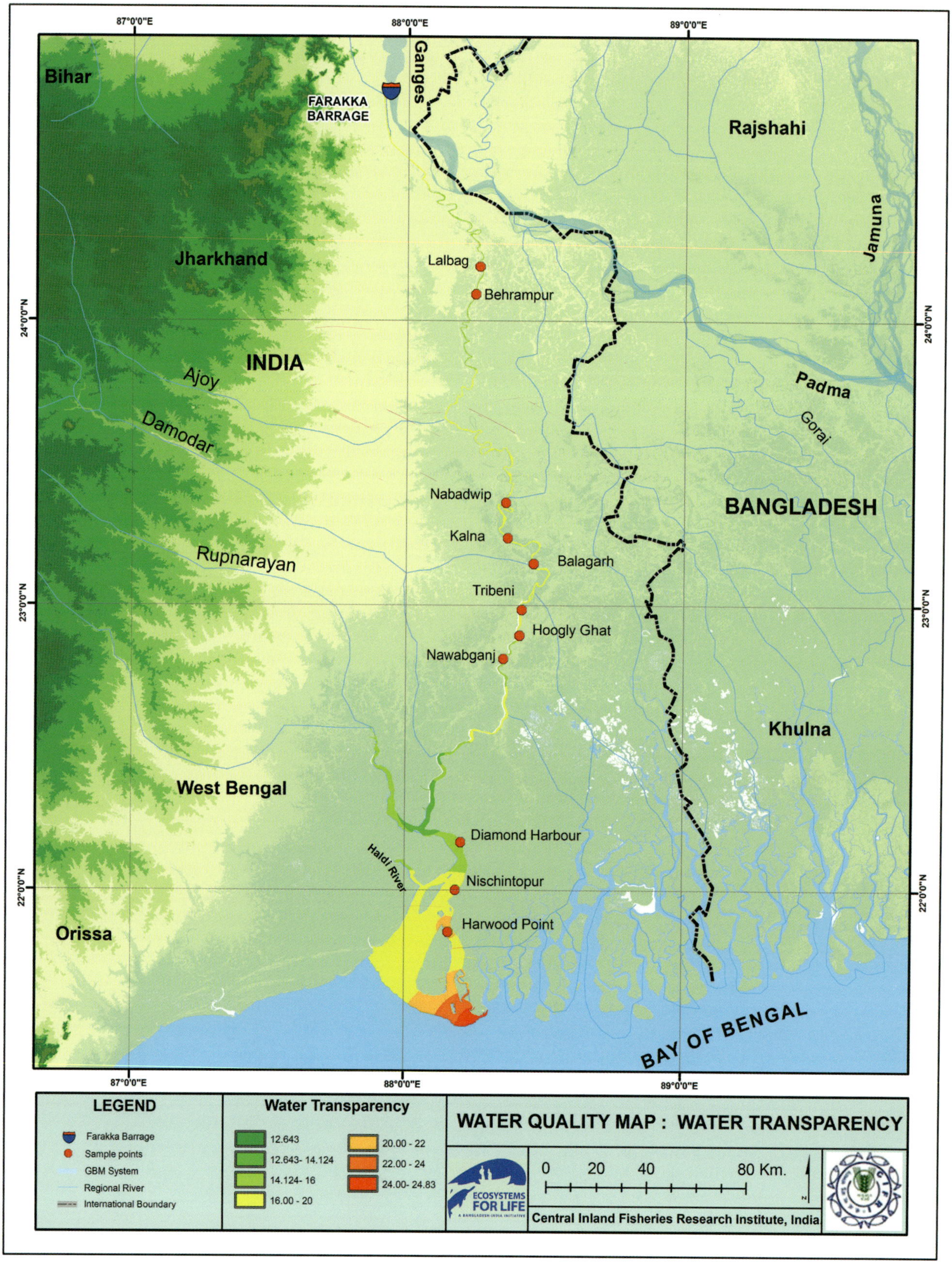

Figure 3.4c

Various Aspects of Hydrological Investigations (Water Chlorophyll)

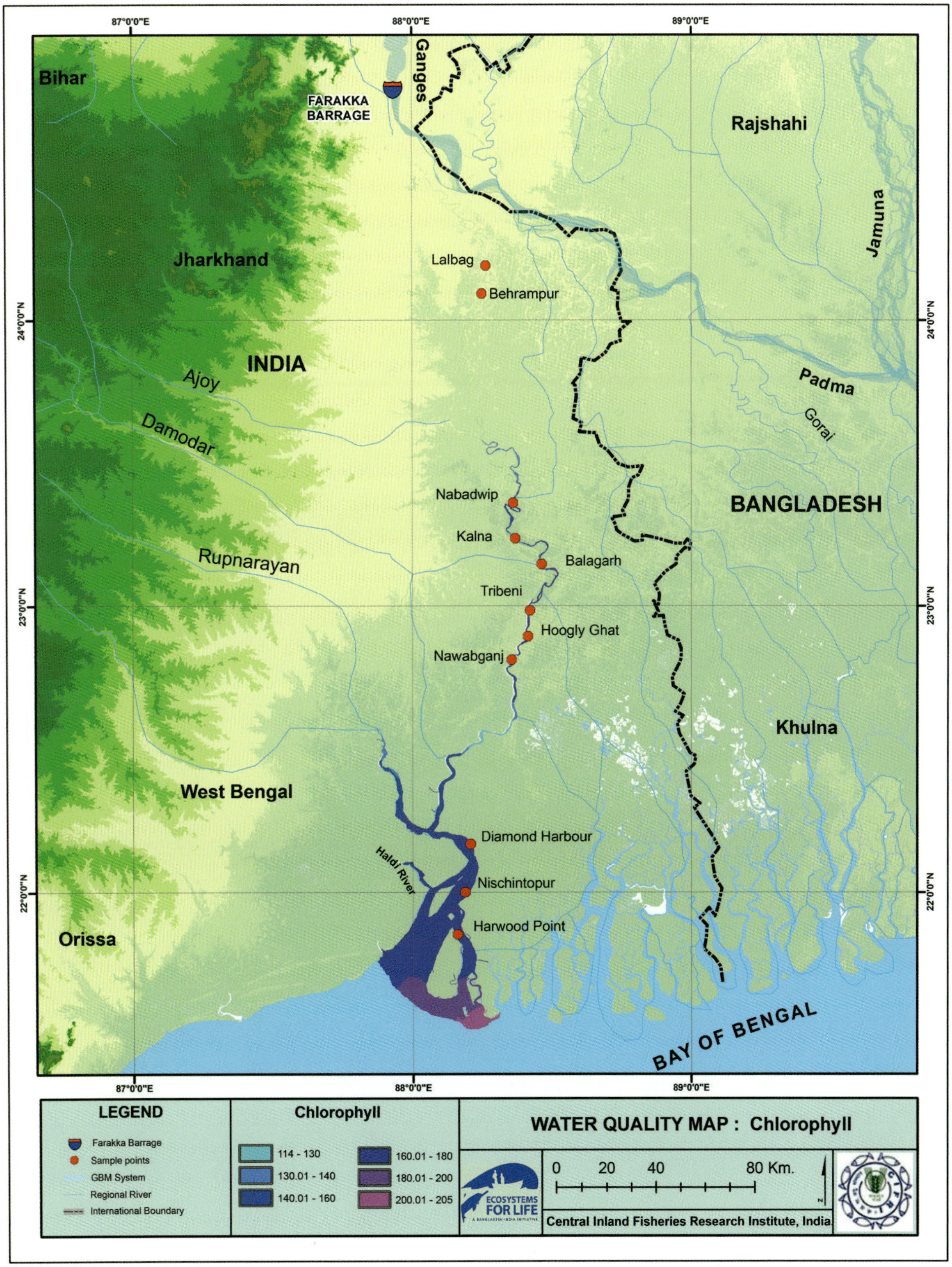

Figure 3.4d

Various Aspects of Hydrological Investigations (Water Salinity)

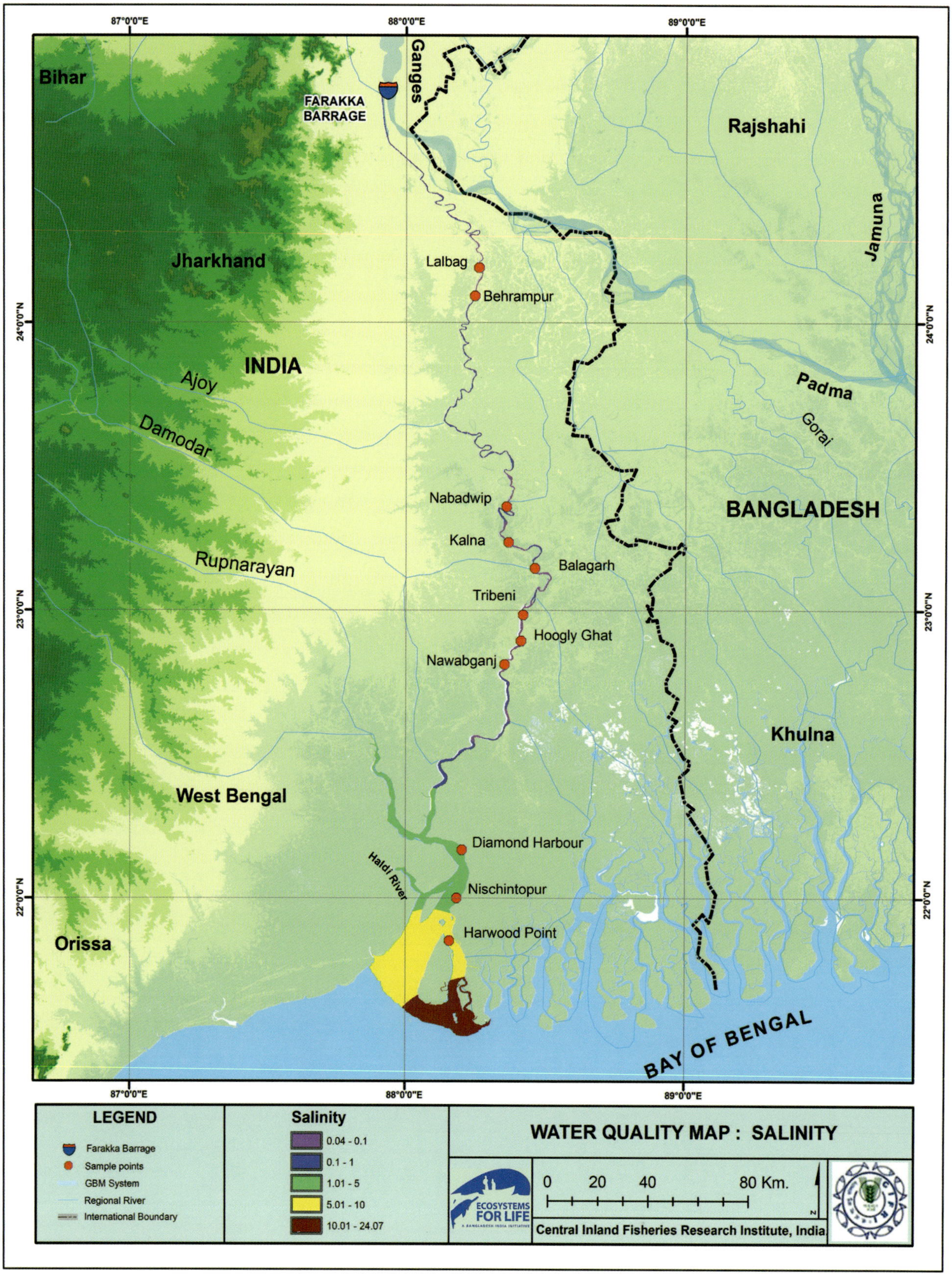

Figure 3.4e

Various Aspects of Hydrological Investigations (Water Turbidity)

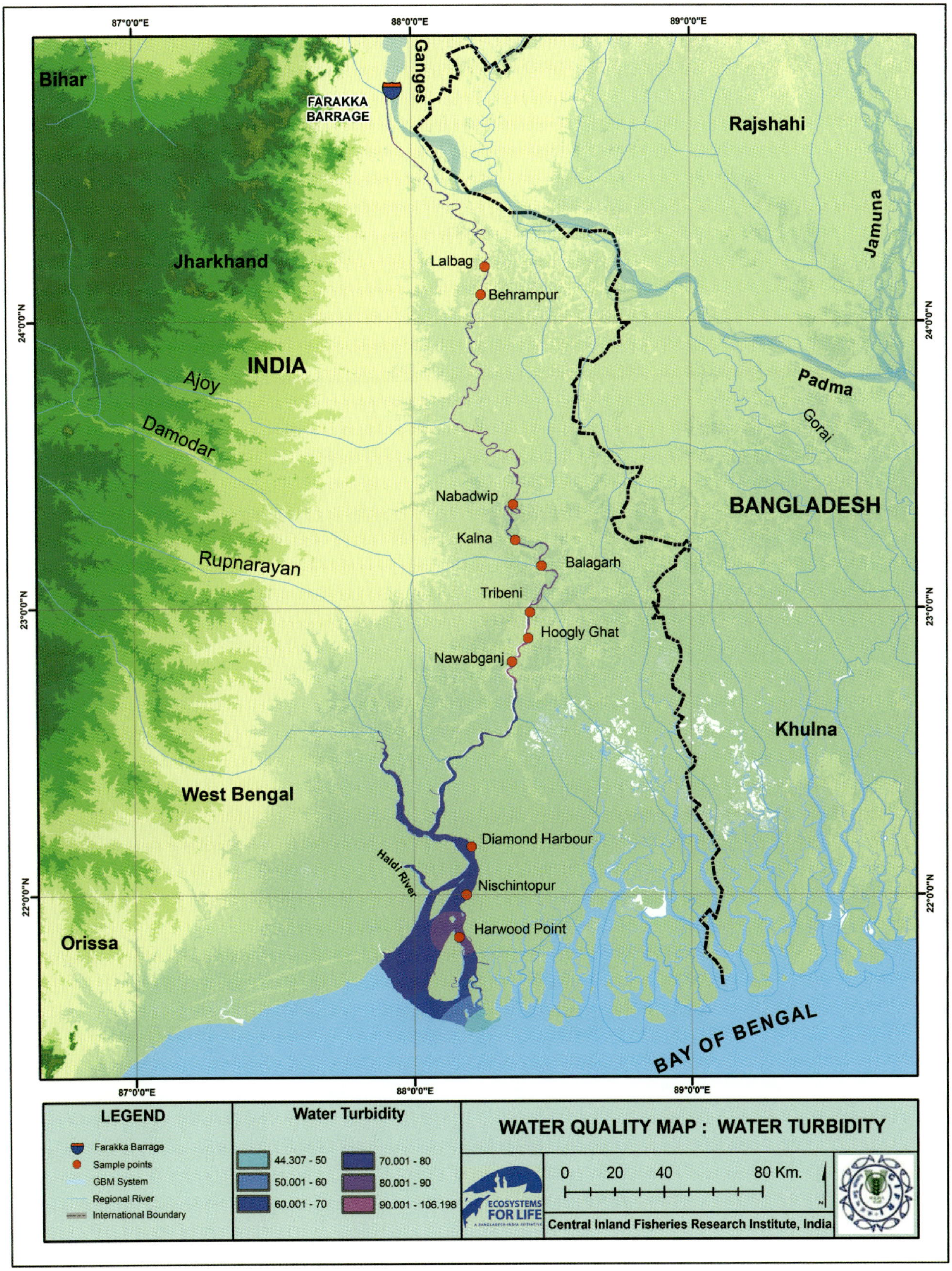

3.2.5 Turbidity

Turbidity of river-estuarine waters (Figure 3.4f) increased by 60-110 per cent following monsoon discharge in July. The value swelled in upper reaches (120-140 NTU) between Farakka and Nawabganj in the initial stage in July. In August, there was a transform in turbidity distribution pattern which was comparatively more between Balagarh and Nawabganj and further down near Godakhali-Harwood point.

3.2.6 Water Temperature

Figure 3.3 indicates that ambient temperature of water ranged between 23.8°C and 33.3°C during April to October 2011 and showed zonal variation. The lower zone recorded comparatively lower temperature (23.8-32.0°C) while it was higher in freshwater tidal zone (29.1-33.3°C). In upper region, the temperature was again low (27.5-32.1°C). Low temperature in lower zone was possibly due to marine influence.

3.2.7 Transparency

Transparency of water decreased following monsoon discharge in the entire stretch of the investigation. Transparency increased in post-monsoon period, which was in favour of high photosynthetic activities and overall improvement in the ecological environment.

3.2.8 Total Suspended Solids

Total suspended solids showed slight variation between surface and bottom in few sampling points. The value was higher in the sea face zone near Frazergunj. At the surface water, value ranged between 0.012 and 3.632 g/l while at the bottom, it ranged between 0.008 and 1.364. Highest value was recorded in Frazergunj site.

3.2.9 Dissolved Oxygen

Figures 3.4 indicate that in general, DO was higher in freshwater zone of Hooghly-Bhagirathi system and the sea facing area. The value of dissolved gas was higher during April and May as compared to other months. Concentration of DO fluctuated within a moderate range of 4.0-7.6 ppm. The level of oxygen ranged between 5.2-7.4 ppm in upper freshwater zone during the period of observations, which indicated higher productivity and congenial environment for migration and nurturing of *Hilsa* in the region.

3.2.10 pH

The water pH (Figure 3.4) ranged between 7.2 and 8.6 thus indicating alkaline environment of the investigated system. Marginal, seasonal variation in pH was observed between seasons and zones. In summer months, water pH was low (7.2-8.0 below Baranagar) as compared to upper reaches (8.2-8.6). With monsoon discharge, the pH increased in lower zone and entire stretch was under uniform alkaline condition (8.0 to 8.3).

3.2.11 Salinity

The salinity of Hooghly estuary remained below 0.05 ppt up to Nishchintpur and below that, chloride concentration enhanced during post-monsoon period. The low salinity was ideal for breeding and nurturing of *Hilsa*. Low salinity facilitates *Hilsa* to breed in freshwater zone of the river system. Further, maximum juveniles of various sites were encountered in the catches in freshwater zones coinciding with breeding seasons. This is in conformity with the study of Bhaumik (2010).

3.2.12 Chlorophyll

Spatio-temporal variation in chlorophyll concentration was noticed during the study period (Figure 3.4c). Chlorophyll concentration in general was more during post-monsoon season and it was comparatively higher at the downstream stretch below Diamond Harbour and upper freshwater tidal zone. The zone of high chlorophyll concentration coincided with nursery grounds of *Hilsa*.

3.3 Threshold Values of Physico-Chemical Parameters for *Hilsa* Migration, Breeding and Rearing in India

Hilsa (*Tenualosa ilisha*) has year round fishery with two distinguished peaks of monsoon and winter in Bhagirathi-Hooghly linkage of Ganga river system. These peaks constitute brood stocks of *Hilsa* with varying maturity stages. The monsoon peak forms of 90-95 per cent matured *Hilsa*, while winter reserves are mixed population of immature and mature fishes. Prolonged and extensive monitoring of migratory and breeding behaviour and rearing grounds of *Hilsa* emerged with some physico-chemical and biological factors which are cumulatively responsible for stimulation and triggering migration of adult *Hilsa* into the system.

The monsoon run-off of huge turbid water above 100 NTU preferably 100-140 NTU turbidity is prime requisite for attracting shoals of brood *Hilsa* to the Hooghly-Bhagirathi system. Depth plays a limited role in the movement of migrating *Hilsa*. Water column of 18-20 m is observed to be ideal for stress-free movement of brood stocks. *Hilsa* fish pass through comparatively lower depth (av. 10 m) in winter months. It is worth mentioning here that the size of migratory *Hilsa* in winter is smaller than that in the monsoon period. Temperature of river-estuarine water was observed to drop by 1.5°C from an average of 31.3°C (29.5-32.6°C) to 29.8°C (29.3-30.2°C) during monsoon migration of brood fishes. On the other hand, in late winter (February) the ambient temperature rises by 1.8°C from average of 27.6°C (26.8-28.4°C) to 28.6°C (27.0-31.8°C) which is thought to cast a spell on upstream migration and breeding of *Hilsa*.

Among chemical factors, salinity plays a determining role in breeding migration of *Hilsa* into the system. Since salinity of the estuarine-river system remains below 0.1 ppt for greater part of the year, migration and breeding activities of *Hilsa* never get hindered within the system. In this system, fishes get alkaline environment (pH 7.7-8.3) during their stay and life span. DO content of the habitat by and large fluctuates in the range of 5.0-7.0 ppm. However, during monsoon, the average oxygen increases by 1.22 ppm from 4.63 ppm to 5.85 ppm.

Chlorophyll values of the river-estuarine system fluctuated between 0.114 and 0.180 µg/l during monsoon period. It was observed that values were comparatively more in some stretches where nursery grounds were located.

While mentioning about threshold values of hydrography and physico-chemical parameters for breeding and nursery activities of *Hilsa*, the conditions given in Table 3.2 were recorded and could be considered ideal for the Hooghly-Bhagirathi river system.

3.4 Biological Aspects in Hooghly River System

3.4.1 Size Distribution

The size and frequency distribution was depicted in Figure 3.5. Predictive population density estimated is overlaid in the histogram. The summary statistics included mean, median, maximum, minimum, standard deviation and coefficient of variation (CV); 95 per cent confidence interval of mean has been depicted in Table 3.3. The predictive population density estimated separately for male and female indicated that overall spread of size

Table 3.2

Threshold Values of Physico-chemical Parameters for *Hilsa* Migration, Breeding and Rearing

	Breeding Activities	*Nursery Activities*
Depth	20 m and above for migration and pre-breeding congregation	Comparatively shallower depth near river-estuarine margins above the congregation grounds
Turbidity (NTU)	100-140	Comparatively low turbid areas (70-80 NTU)
Temperature (°C)	29.3-30.2	29.8-30.8
Salinity (ppt)	<0.1	<0.1
DO (ppm)	5.0-6.8	4.8-6.8
pH	7.70-8.30	7.9-8.40
Chlorophyll (µg/l)	0.114-0.180	0.140-0.180

Table 3.3

Sex-wise Summary Statistics of Size of *Hilsa*

Statistics	*Length (mm)*		*Weight (gm)*	
	Male	*Female*	*Male*	*Female*
Mean	287 (285,290)*	321 (319,323)*	277 (273,281)*	362 (356, 370)*
Median	284	292	260	296
Standard deviation	25.7	40.1	85.5	205.6
Maximum	425	525	780	1700
Minimum	207	206	140	110
CV (%)	8.9	12.5	30.9	56.8

Note: * The values within parenthesis are 95 per cent confidence interval of mean.

Figure 3.5

Sex-wise Observed and Predictive Size Distribution of *Hilsa*

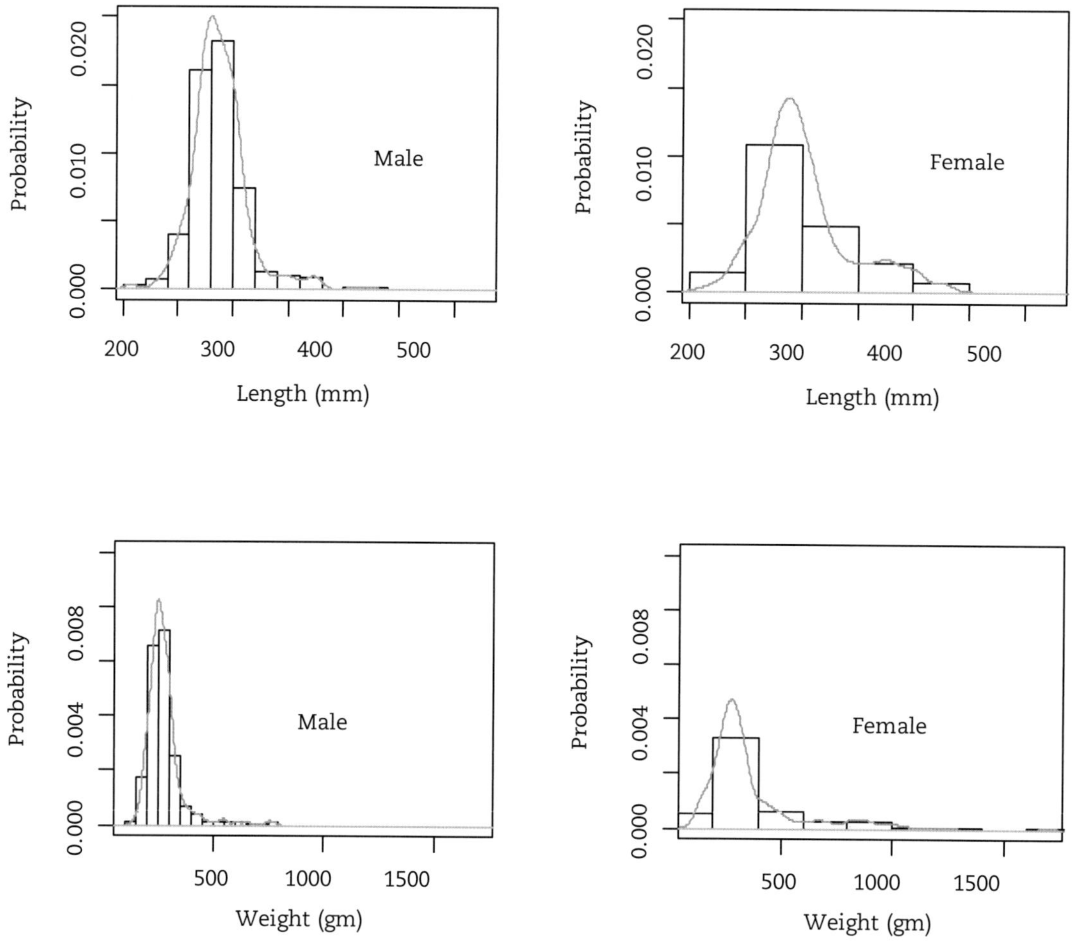

distribution of female was more than that of male. Female size distribution in terms of length and weight was more skewed than size distribution of male. This indicated that chance of getting larger sized fish of female variety was more than that of male. Comparing standard deviation and CV (%), it could be concluded that female population was more variable in size than male. Variability in weight was more than that in length, for both male and female; 50 per cent of male and female fishes were of length below 284 mm and 292 mm (median length) respectively and 50 per cent of male and female fish were of weight below 260 gm and 296 gm (median weight) respectively.

3.4.2 Length Weight Relationship: Sex Ratio

To get an idea about changes in sex ratio at size (Figure 3.6), the entire samples were divided into four groups of equal sizes on the basis of four quartiles in the observed weight distribution. The sex ratio (male: female) expressed in percentage form was computed for each group and presented in Table 3.4. The overall sex ratio found was 42:58 (male: female) which is significantly (p-value < 0.05) different from 50:50. The 95 per cent confidence interval of male proportion is 0.36 to 0.41 which is far below 0.5. Both of these findings indicate that *Hilsa* population is female-dominated.

As part of empirical evidence of changing sex ratio at size, the sex ratio of different age groups has been depicted in Figure 3.7. It was observed that sex ratio changes from size groups 280 gm to 340 gm and it drastically changes to 18:82 (male: female) in the size group of more than 340 gm. The statistical test (equality of proportion) ensured significant (p-value < 0.05) differences of male proportion among different size groups. The above investigation portrayed only the evidence of changing sex ratios at size on the basis of sample observations.

3.4.3 Gonado-somatic Index

Maturity stages *i.e.*, gonado-somatic index (GSI) of the migrating spawners of *Hilsa* varied with season and location. Advanced stages of female *Hilsa* appeared first in the lower stretch around Nishchintpur in July. In August, the distribution of gravid *Hilsa* was wider and their concentration was more in upper freshwater tidal zone

Figure 3.6

Distribution of Sex Ratio

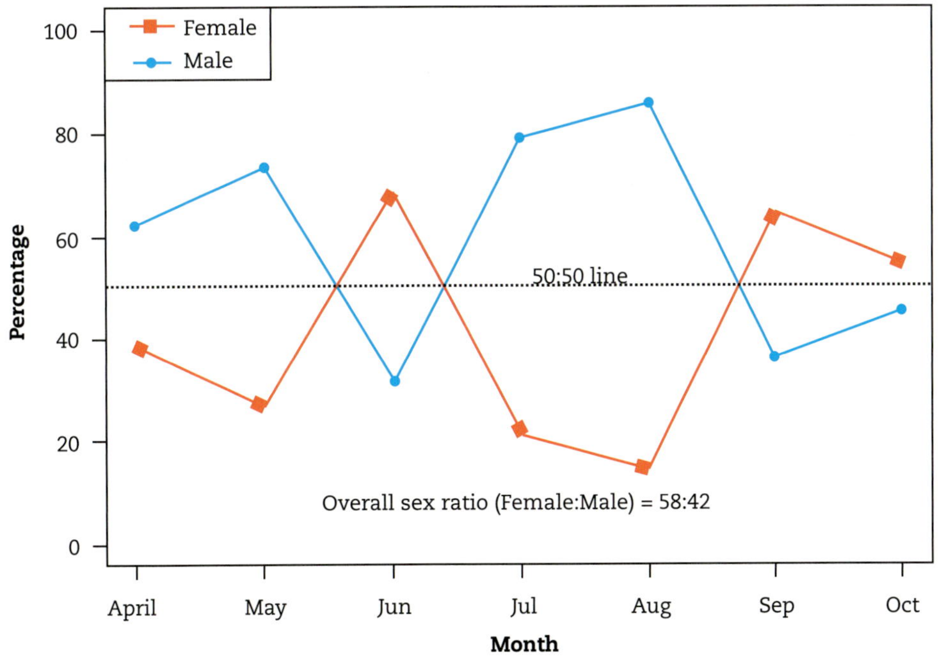

Table 3.4

Sex Ratio and Frequency Over Different Size Group

Weight group (gm)	*Male*	*Female*	*Total*	*Male:Female (in %)*
<239.5	130	141	271	48:52
239.5–280	140	132	272	51:49
280–340	96	149	267	36:64
>340	49	220	269	18:82
Total	415	664	1079	38:62

Figure 3.7

Sex Ratios of Different Size Group

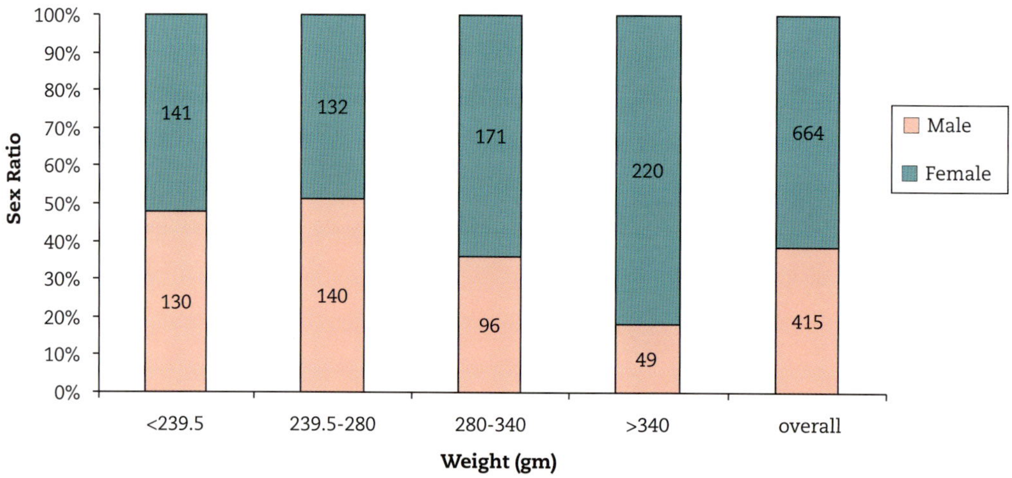

between Hooghly Ghat and Balagarh and in comparatively lower intensity below Farakka in Bhagirathi system. For the first time, a female *Hilsa* of 105 g was found in 5th stage of maturity from lower stretch of the estuary in late monsoon period.

The study in the estuarine and marine part, however, observed an increasing trend of predominance of females over males. During 29th August, male:female ratio was found to be 1:1.03 which increased consistently up to 1:1.16 during 12th October, indicating predominance of females during spawning. Over time, a gradual decrease in predominance of females was observed and it was found to be 1:1.07 during 10th December lunar cycle.

GSI values of female *Hilsa* in lower estuarine part showed a steady increase from 29th August to 12th October, i.e., 1.69 to 4.83 respectively and a sharp fall on 26th October sample (1.92) (Figure 3.8) indicating second spawning during 12th October lunar cycle. Afterwards a gradual rise in GSI values was observed that reached up to 2.39 during 10th December lunar cycle. Hossain (1985) studied the GSI of female *Hilsa* in three environments, *viz.*, freshwater, estuarine and marine habitats, for each month. He observed that there were three peaks in GSI values for Meghna *Hilsa*, in October, June and February. GSI values of estuarine *Hilsa* showed two peaks, one in March, another in June. His 'estuarine' sample came from Barisal, where landings are a combination of riverine, estuarine and marine *Hilsa*. On the other hand, values of marine *Hilsa* exhibited rise of GSI starting in June and reaching a peak in August. A small ascent of value was noted in February with a downward slope in March. Findings of present study are thus in close conformity with observations of Hossain, with an additional observation of peaking of GSI value in October.

3.4.4 *Frequency of Egg Diameter in the Lower Estuary*

The maturation of female *Hilsa* was studied to determine the period of spawning. The progression of ova into full maturity from I to VI stages (as discussed in earlier chapter) and partially spent and spent stages (VII and VIII) were well depicted by ova size frequencies. From the last week of August to 2nd week of December, all stages of maturity were found in catches. During the last week of August, ova diameters of more than 0.6 mm which is presumed to be mature were 22.38 ± 3.57 per cent. Occurrence of such matured ova increased up to 39.21 ± 4.98 per cent during 12th October full moon lunar cycle. In the next lunar cycle occurrence of such ova decreased down to 19.35 ± 5.26 per cent. This was thus a clear indication of major spawning during 12th October lunar cycle. Later, percentage of matured ova showed gradual increase almost like GSI and reached up to 25.43 per cent during 10th December lunar cycle. Percentage of ova exceeding 0.6 mm diameter in females is presented in Figure 3.8.

3.4.5 *Juvenile Population*

Occurrence of early stages or juveniles offers evidence of a likely spawning season and spawning ground. Earlier studies indicated that *Hilsa* bred year-round with seasonal peaks (June-July, October and February) in almost all the major rivers. Abundance of *Hilsa* larvae/fry was studied in all the stations deploying *Meen Jaal* during every lunar cycle within the study period.

In the Hooghly, according to Hora (1938), the brood of July-August was believed to attain a length of 140-150 mm by the third week of November, indicating growth during first four months. Hora and Nair (1940a) recorded a length of 40-50 mm, 80-89 mm, 100 mm, 130 mm, and 160 mm during first successive five-month period; they also estimated an average increase of 30 mm per month during the first five months, and 20 mm per month for next seven months. A slower growth rate of 35 mm a month during November and a higher rate of 50 mm per month during summer months were observed. From rivers of Bangladesh, they have recorded juveniles of 50-79 mm and 110-129 mm in February and remarked that *jatka* (juvenile of *Hilsa*) came up the rivers in that region towards the end of March. Hora and Nair (1940b) confirmed the identity of *jatka* as juveniles of *Hilsa* and recorded from February to May, a size range of 85-164 mm, which according to them corresponded to an age of two to five months.

They also observed that juveniles migrated from estuaries into the freshwater region for feeding, and during April-May, feeding was stopped and growth inhibited. Jones and Menon (1951) found that in the Chilka Lake, the July-August brood grew to about 110-133 mm by the first week of December. This indicated slower rate of growth as compared to Hora's observation (1938).

Figure 3.8

Percentage of Ova Exceeding 0.6 mm Diameter

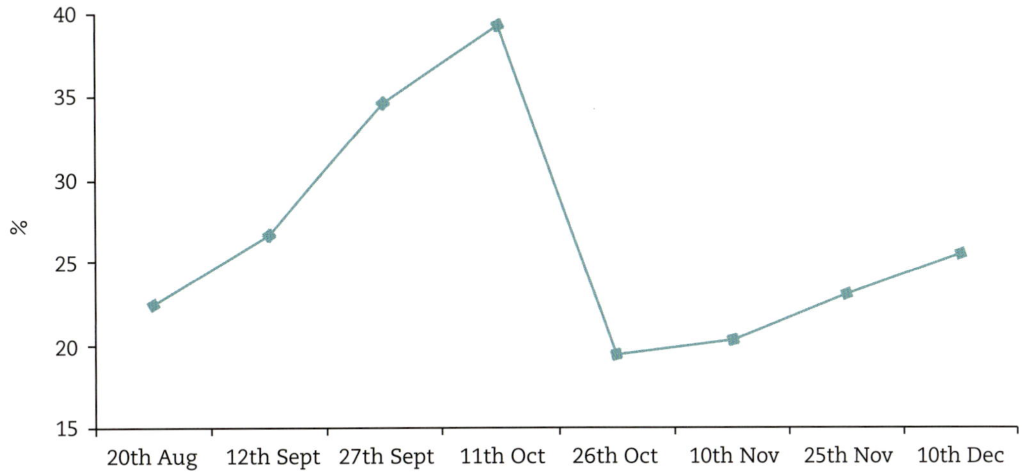

Table 3.5

Abundance of Juvenile (per sq m Net Area per Day) *Hilsa* in Different Stations

	29th Aug	12th Sept	27th Sept	11th Oct	26th Oct	10th Nov	25th Nov	10th Dec
(Station-1)	2.39	1.98	2.15	1.73	1.68	7.56	5.43	6.18
(Station-2)	1.73	1.84	1.56	1.49	1.43	6.98	7.22	4.77
(Station-3)	1.17	1.32	1.28	1.51	1.22	4.39	3.82	2.61
(Station-4)	0.65	0.73	0.48	0.60	0.39	2.98	3.27	3.65
(Station-5)	0.55	0.46	0.53	0.32	0.18	1.76	2.19	2.32

Sujansingani (1957) concluded from records after experimenting with river Hooghly that in the first month, after hatching, fish grows up to 28 mm and in subsequent 2-3 months, it grows at the rate of 15 to 20 mm per month, which slows down to 10 mm per month. Pillay and Rosa (1963) suggested a model size of 65 mm in the river Godavari in January which they traced to 95 mm in February, 125 mm in March, and 155 mm in May. Another model group at 75 mm in March was traced to 115 mm in May. Pillay (1958) recorded a growth of 110-120 mm in three months in respect of Hooghly stocks. In Chilka Lake, Jhingran and Natarajan (1973) assigned the age of the juvenile *Hilsa* measuring 50-74 mm, abundant in December-January, to two months. Ramakrishnaiah (1972) indicated the model size of 62 mm found in December to be the progeny from late monsoon breeding in November which progressed to 137 mm after 5 months: he estimated an average growth of 20 cm during the first year. He was of the opinion that juveniles of 31-90 mm recruited during November-January remain in the lake. Rajyalakshmi (1973) was of the opinion that winter recruits added 100 mm during a period of 4 months (February to June). She also traced the growth of monsoon recruits from 88.5 mm in November to 213.5 mm in June, spanning a period of 7 months.

Records indicated that juveniles remained in rivers/estuaries till they probably reached a length of 150-160 mm which is believed to be attained in 5 months. It is possible that the seaward migration happens at this size/age. No information is available on the rate of survival of early stages of fish, but it was observed that the operation of small-mesh nets in the period immediately succeeding breeding season in the river Hooghly resulted in large-scale destruction of young fish (Pillay and Rosa, 1963). Similar observations were also made with respect to Bangladesh waters by Qureshi (1968).

In our study, mean length of *Hilsa* juveniles was found to be 37 mm, 56 mm, 73 mm, 85 mm and 94 mm in successive lunar cycle starting from 26th August to 26th October indicating another peak spawning during July-August. In the sample stock of 26th October, a sharp increase in number of *Hilsa* post-larvae/juveniles (10-20 mm) in all stations provided further proof of major spawning during 12th October lunar cycle. The model size of *Hilsa* fry was found to be 16.35, 27.88, 39.46 an 40.19 mm during 26th October to 10th December lunar cycle. Abundance of *Hilsa* juveniles (Table 3.5) was highest in Sagar Island (Station-1) and Frasergunj (Station-2), moderate in Kakdwip (Station-3) and lowest in Canning (Station-4) and Gathkhali (Station-5) samples confirming the location of spawning ground at the confluence of Hooghly river. According to a semi-structured interview with fishermen, few other spawning grounds were thought to exist in the lower estuarine area of Matla-Bidya-Raimangal (Ichamti) estuarine complex close to submerged sands of 2-3 meter water depth. Increasing trend in number of *Hilsa* juveniles in Stations 4 and 5 indicated possibility of existence of other spawning grounds at the confluence of Matla-Bidya-Raimangal complex. After hatching, juveniles might have migrated upward for grazing, resulting in an increasing trend in number. However, this needs to be confirmed by detailed surveys and data collection in estuarine-marine area.

Figure 3.9

Month-wise Length Weight Variation of *Hilsa*

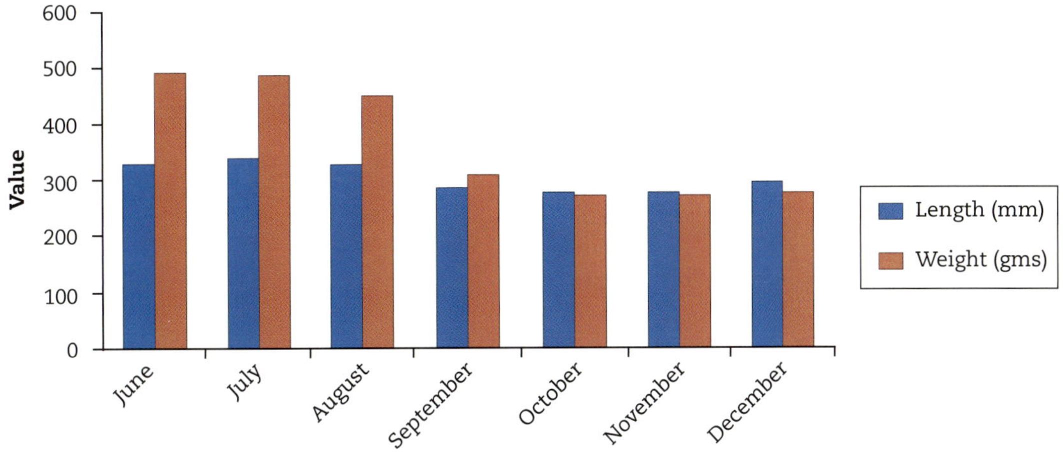

3.4.6 Length-Weight Relationship Study to Assess Health of Fish Stock

The length-weight relationship (LWR) is a very important parameter to understand the growth dynamics of the fish population. Length and weight data are useful standard results of fish sampling programmes (Morato *et al.*, 2001). LWR of fishes are important in fisheries biology because they allow estimation of average weight of fish of a given length group by establishing a mathematical relation between the two parameters (Beyer, 1987). The LWR is particularly important in parameterising yield equations and in estimations of stock size (Abdurahiman *et al.*, 2004). The exact relationship between length and weight differs among species of fish according to their inherited body shape, and within a species according to the condition (robustness) of individual fish (Schneider, 2000). The study of morphometric characters in fishes is important because they can be used for differentiation of taxonomic units (Ambily and Nandan, 2010). A similar study was conducted by Harission *et al.* (2000) Volvich *et al.* (2001), Ecoutin *et al.* (2005), Kalayci *et al.* (2007), Muto *et al.* (2000) and Rahman *et al.* (2004).

In the present study, LWR was calculated along with minimum and maximum length (in mm) and weight (in gram) of *Hilsa* shad from the main marine fish landing centres of Sundarban, West Bengal. Total length was measured from the lower jaw to the tip of the tail, spread normally (Volvich and Appelbaum, 2001).

The mean length data, however, showed that the mean length of October catch was much less compared to June-August. Month-wise length-weight variation is shown in Figure 3.9. In June and July, the mean length-weight of *Hilsa* was close to being same, but after July, it decreased and was minimum in October. Weight was much more than the length of *Hilsa* in June to August, but weight and length of *Hilsa* were found to be the same in September and November. Length exhibited a slight increase in December.

The LWR was established by the equation $W=a.L^b$ (Le Cren, 1951), where W is the weight of the fish, L is the total length of the fish, 'a' is the exponent describing rate of change of weight with respect to length and 'b' denotes weight at unit length; 'a' and 'b' were also calculated from $W=a.L^b$ equation.

When parameter b is equal to 3, the growth is called isometric but the growth is allometric when value of 'b' is more or less than 3. From the study of LWR of 433 *Hilsa* specimens taken at random, it was observed that during the study period (June-December, 2011), length and weight of *Hilsa* varied between 208 mm and 488 mm, 94.1 g and 1382.3 g respectively. The value of 'b' *Hilsa* was 2.866 and value of r^2 was 0.9093. The LWR of *Hilsa* is $W = 0.00002{*}L^{2.866}$ (Figure 3.14). Thus, growth of *Hilsa* was found to be close to allometric from this limited period of study. Reuben *et al.* (1992) established the LWR of *Hilsa* from northeast coast of India and the relationship was W

Figure 3.10

Migration Patterns of *Hilsa*

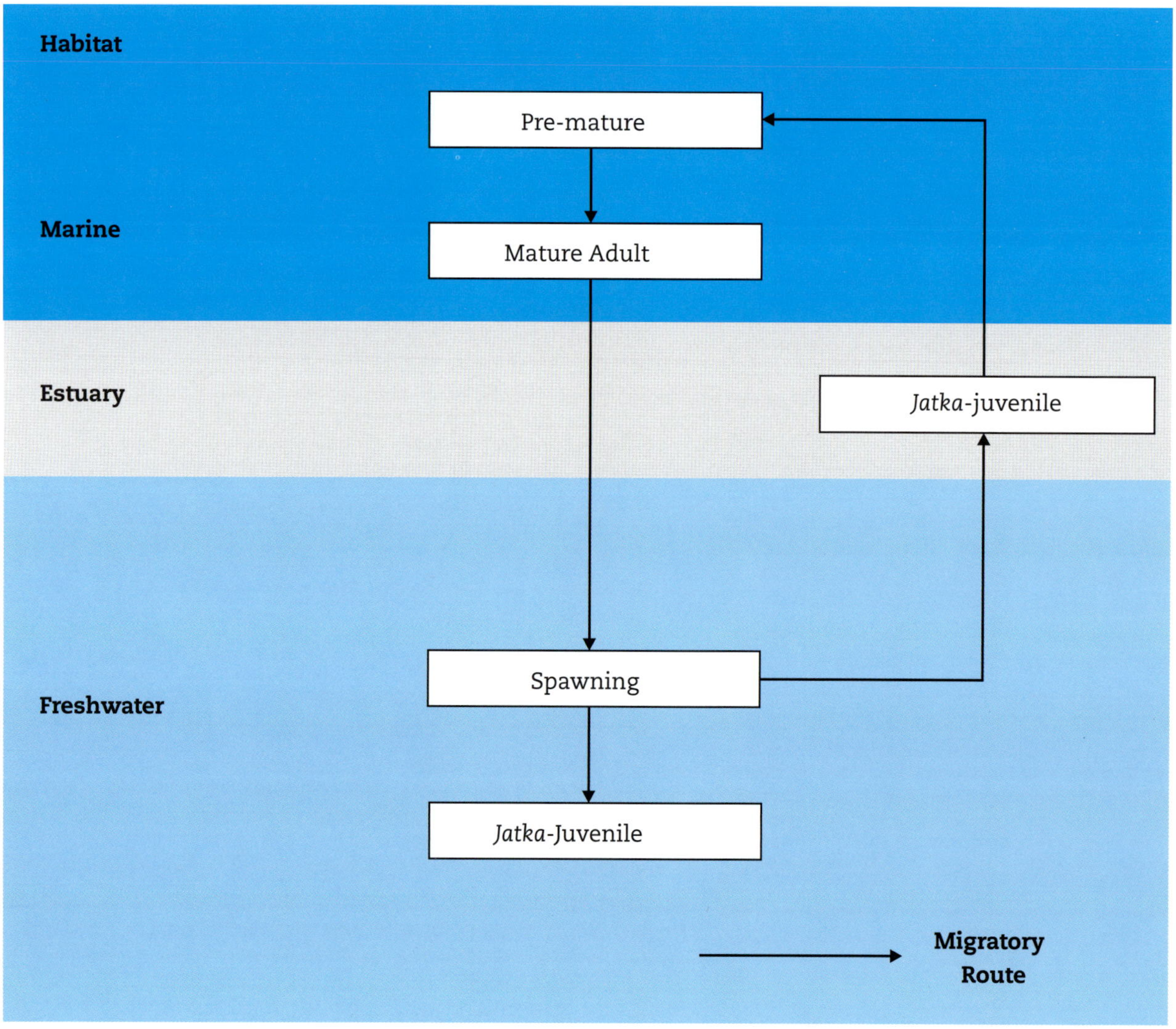

= $0.00003693321*L^{2.8053}$. The LWR of *Hilsa* W = $0.00305*TL^{3.381}$ was calculated by Amin *et al.* (2005) from Bangladesh water. Thus, in general, health of the *Hilsa* shad was found to be normal and not under any severe environmental stress.

3.5 Migration Pattern

3.5.1 Migration of Hilsa in Meghna River System

Hilsa shad (*T. ilisha*) is anadromous in nature, i.e., capable of withstanding a wide range of salinity and migrating long distance from marine habitat to up-stream freshwater. *Hilsa* lives in the sea for most of its life but migrates to inland freshwater through rivers in Indian sub-continent for spawning (Figure 3.10).

3.5.2 Migration in Padma River System

Hilsa starts spawning migration upstream during the southwest monsoon and consequent flooding of all rivers (Rahman, 2005). The eggs are deposited in freshwater and hatching takes place within 23-26 hours at an average temperature of 23°C. Larvae and juveniles make their way downstream to the sea during a period of 5-6 months. They feed and grow *en route*. In about 6-10 weeks, fry grows to about 12-20 cm and becomes known as *jatka*. At this stage, they start migration to the sea for further growth and maturity. After growing for a year in the sea, *Hilsa* become mature and their spawning migration towards inland rivers begins thus continuing the cycle (Haroon, 1998). *Hilsa* is relatively fecund. Numbers of eggs are found to be 144 thousand in 28 cm long fish up to 2.3 million in 44.5 cm long fish. The peak-breeding period of *Hilsa* is placed during the full moon in October (Halder, 2004).

The *Hilsa* is known to be a fast swimmer (Southwell and Prashad, 1918). Thus distances of 50-100 km migration is usual and normal in Bangladesh rivers. *Hilsa* may reach up to 60 cm in total length, but commonly found specimens measure 35-40 cm. A large-sized *Hilsa* weighs about 2.5 kg. Some conflicting views have been expressed on minimum size of *Hilsa* at first maturity. Day (1878) observed that *Hilsa* may attain first maturity at the end of the first year or at the beginning of the second year. In Bangladesh waters (Meghna River), Quddus and Shafi (1983) observed that, the size at first maturity is 21 cm in case of males and 32 cm in the case of females.

The spawning migration towards estuaries and rivers starts from July till October, also from January to February/March. During this migratory period, the catch percentage of *Hilsa* from inland rivers is very high, and 80 per cent of females are found in egg-releasing condition to support the spawning status of the fish (Shafi and Quddus, 1982). After breeding, juveniles of *Hilsa/jatka*, from 4-15 cm, are abundant from February to May in the foreshore and riverine waters of Bangladesh's deltaic rivers, including Padma and Meghna (Rahman, 2001). After growing 1-2 years in sea, the fish matures and reaches a size of 32-35 cm prior to their spawning migration towards inland rivers, and life-cycle continues (Quddus and Shafi, 1983). By plotting the *Hilsa* catch by fishers along the river side (DoF, 2011), the figure shows the recent migratory pattern of *Hilsa* fish (Figure 3.11).

3.5.3 Migration of Hilsa in Bhagirathi-Hooghly River System

Indian shad, *Tenualosa ilisha* migrates to freshwater environment of the river systems for breeding followed by nourishment of young ones. Breeding success of species depends on synchronous effect of eco-environmental and biological conditions (Bhaumik and Sharma, 2011). The fish normally inhabits the lower region of estuaries and foreshore areas of the sea. *Hilsa* prefers to reside in this region due to presence of sub-surface oxygen, relatively low salinity, strong tidal action, high turbidity, heavy siltation and rich growth of plankton (Pillay and Rosa, 1963). It is well known that *Hilsa* ascends rivers for spawning (Hora, 1938; Pillay, 1958; De, 1986; Bhaumik *et al.*, 2011a) and their progeny migrate down the river towards lower estuaries and coastal areas (Pillay, 1958). Most of the stocks of *Hilsa* are anadromous, breeding much above tidal limits (Naidu, 1939). Some stocks have also been reported to remain permanently in freshwater stretch of rivers (Hora, 1938; Hora and Nair, 1940) and some spawn in tidal areas. There is no doubt that *Hilsa* is very salinity tolerant and inhabits freshwater, estuarine and coastal waters in the Bay of Bengal.

Figure 3.11

***Hilsa* Migration in Bangladesh**

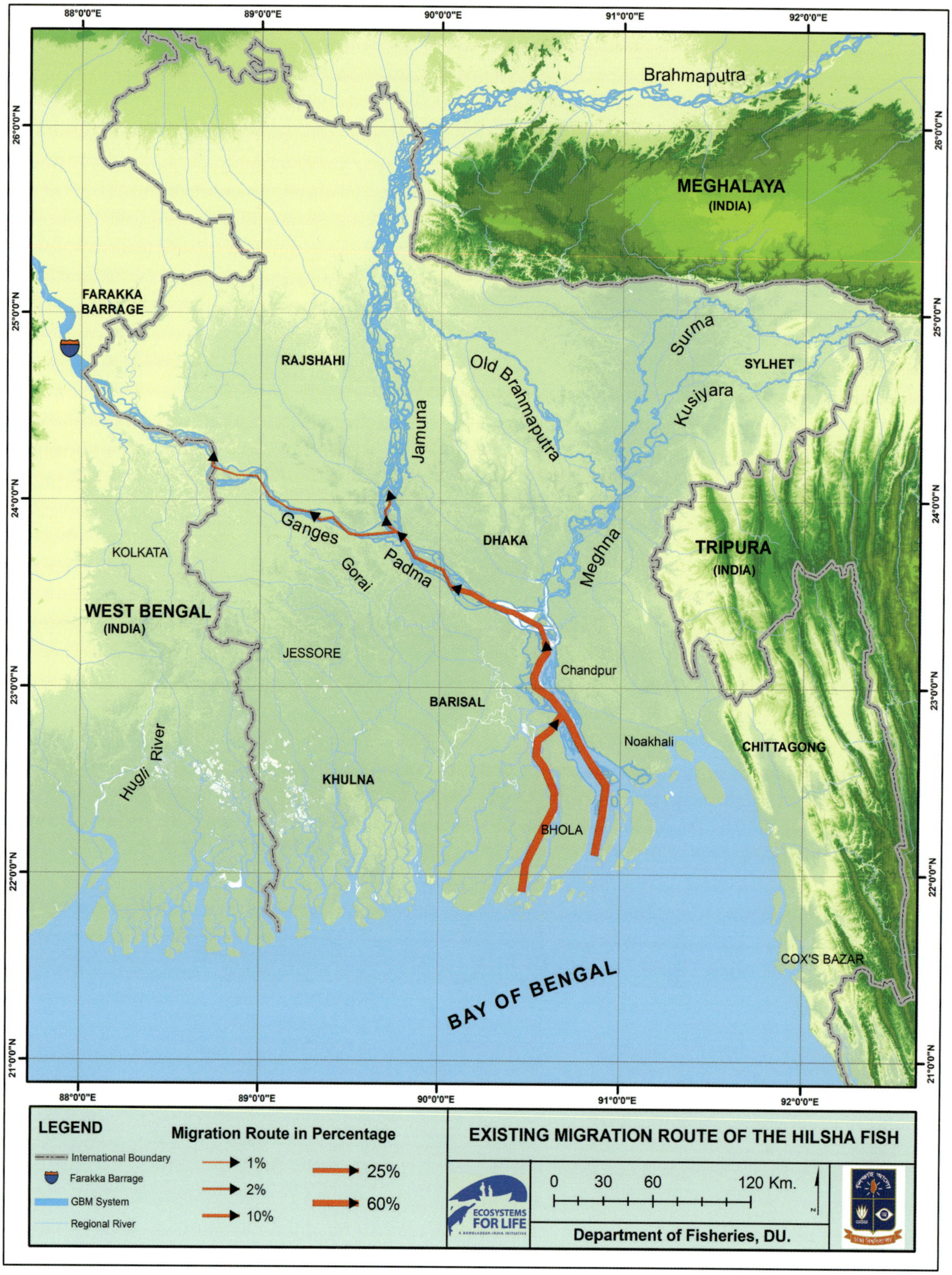

Source: DoF, 2011.

It has been observed that *Hilsa* move on the surface in the foreshore region, whereas in the river, they move in deeper zones (Bhaumik, 2010). The species move in shoals. The peak upstream migration of *Hilsa* in most of the rivers of the country generally commensurates with southwest monsoon i.e., months of July and August and continues to October-November. In the Hooghly estuary, period of migration is found to be prolonged and extended up to February. A wide range of pattern of upstream migration of the fish in various river systems of the country has been reported.

Regarding migration of *Hilsa* into the Hooghly-Bhagirathi estuary, it was observed that the fish ascends only for spawning and their progeny generally after attainment of a size range of 80-110 mm start their downstream migration towards coastal region which commences from February and continues to June. The young *Hilsa*, after leaving rivers, do not go far into the sea but move about in shoals in the estuary and foreshore regions.

Earlier studies indicated that in the past (pre-Farakka barrage period), the *Hilsa* of the Ganga river system used to migrate up to Agra, Kanpur and Delhi in years of excessive abundance, while in normal years, the fish used to migrate up to Allhabad, where maximum abundance was observed up to Buxar region (Figure 3.12).

The upstream migration was observed to be associated mainly with the state of sexual maturity as well as volume of freshwater discharge from the estuary during monsoon. However, other factors like rainfall, current velocity and temperature, low salinity, turbidity, primary productivity and availability of planktonic food cannot be ignored (Bhaumik and Sharma, 2011).

The migratory movement of *Hilsa* into and from the river was studied in the Hooghly river at Diamond Harbour and marine zone of the estuary off Frazerganj. Fishing of *Hilsa* by gill net was observed during January to March and June to November. The direction of entangling of the fish i.e., towards river or sea, and position of entangling in the net i.e., at the top, centre or bottom of the net was recorded. The sex, maturity and length of fish caught during days of investigation on board fishing vessel were recorded. It was observed that a large number of *Hilsa* was entangled in the gill net at the top and central portion during high tide especially in the evening hours during their migration process into the river. On the contrary, during low tide migrating, spent fishes from river into the sea were invariably gilled at the bottom of the net indicating habitat of the spent fish. Experimental fishing to follow movements of *Hilsa* was conducted during peak periods of migration in monsoon, post monsoon and winter. As compared to the higher catch of *Hilsa* in the coastal areas and the lower estuary, poor catch was recorded in the river which indicated that *Hilsa* does not move in the river in shoals.

Based on the study of extensive samples of fish for length, frequency, sex ratio and maturity, condition of the migrants, etc., it was observed that there were two well-marked migration patterns of *Hilsa* into the Hooghly: one during monsoon (May-October) and the other during the winter (January-February). In the riverine area, large groups of fish are abundant between May and October. Post-October, these groups begin declining and reach a minimum by December. Catch rates for the Hooghly revealed two peaks, one in May and another in August. A medium-sized group was available all throughout the year. From November to March, medium-sized groups showed dominance over large-sized groups. During this time, fishermen fished using smaller-meshed nets, because of the predominance of smaller- to medium-sized *Hilsa*. The catch rate and GSI value were found to be higher during March. The catch rate of this medium-sized fish in winter indicated lesser degree of migration into the river. Two size groups of 285-323 mm and 300-430 mm, former being the most dominant, participated in spring migration. The monsoon run of *Hilsa* comprised of two groups varying between 300-370 mm and 400-500 mm, the later being the most dominant occurring. Smaller size fish of less than 285 mm entered the river sporadically in very small numbers along with bigger size groups of spring and monsoon runs of *Hilsa*. The spring spawners that enter the river for spawning in January-March return to the sea during July-August when these are caught in good numbers. The monsoon spawners that enter the river during September-October return to the sea after spawning and these spent

Figure 3.12

Migration Route of *Hilsa* During Pre-Farakka Period

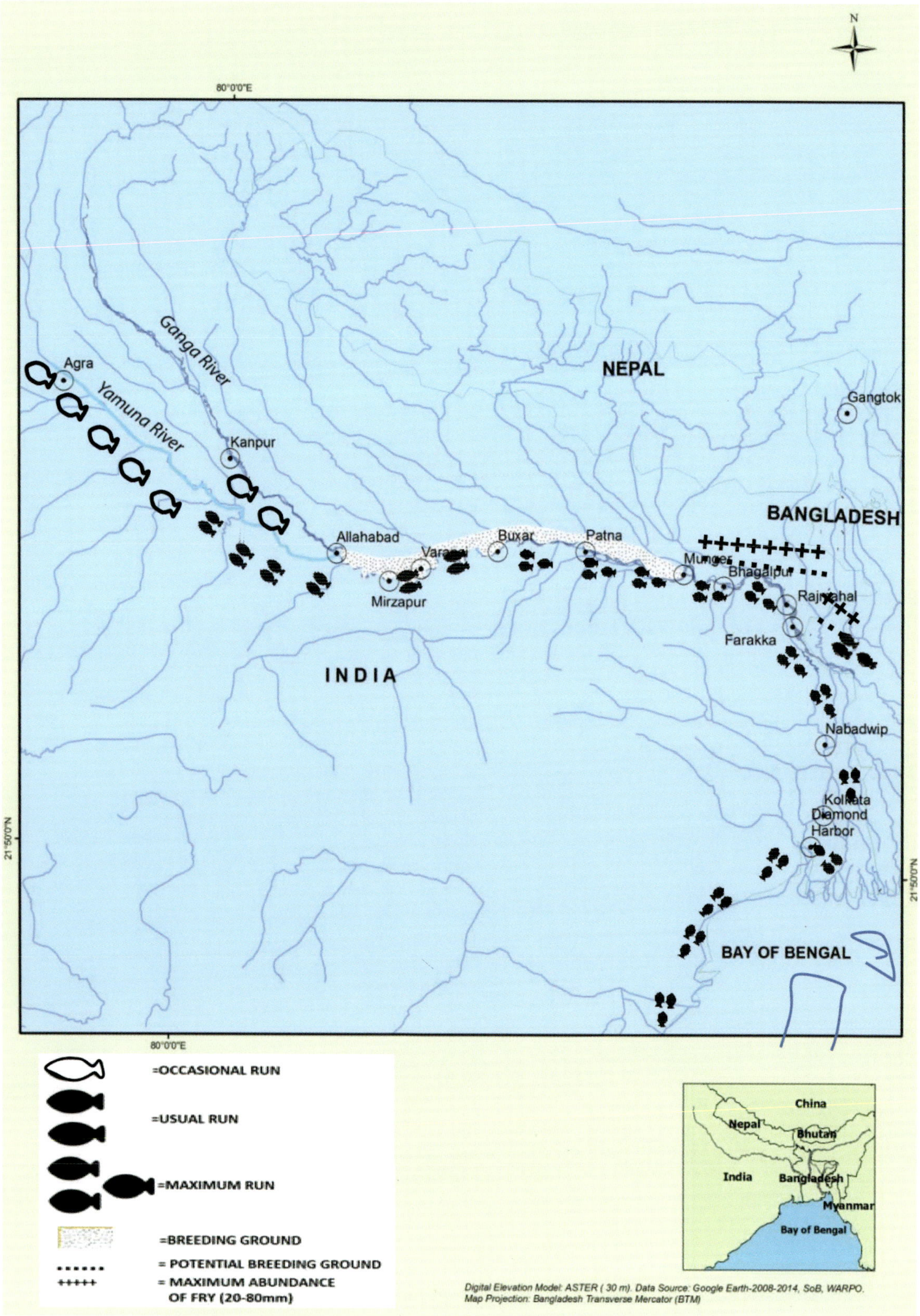

Source: De, 2001.

fishes are caught in good numbers during January-March. Similarly, the offspring of spring spawners make a journey towards the sea from the river during November-January, whereas the offsprings of monsoon spawners return to the sea from the river during July-September. The return of the broods of spring and monsoon spawners to the sea is not as precise as the river-ward migration of *Hilsa*. Full recruitment of juveniles into the marine fishery is observed for 4-5 months in a year i.e., between July and January with a peak in October. The minimum size at recruitment into the sea is at 160-180 mm, whereas juveniles are fully recruited into the fishery at a length of 260-270 mm approximately at an age of 1 year. But the maximum exploitation of this stock is affected when they congregate in the near shore areas and lower estuaries at lengths of 300-390 mm at the age of about 2 years (approximately). This also coincides with the size at first maturity of *Hilsa*. It was observed that migration of *Hilsa* takes place in large numbers only when water depth, current velocity, volume of discharge stimulating flood pulse and temperature are favourable for them.

The upstream migration of winter spawners and the downstream migration of summer spawners as spent fish are likely to intermingle at various positions in one or other environment. Such intermingling cannot be ignored owing to the use of different mesh sizes in fishing operations.

It has further been observed that some young *Hilsa* stocks appear to remain in the freshwater zones throughout the year as per the record of regular catches. It puts forth a question for these populations towards its migration strategy. Similar observations (whether such population is truly anadromous) were also made by Pillay and Rosa (1963), but it calls for further investigation.

The depth of the river (Figure 3.13) and *Hilsa* catch have a direct correlation. At the mouth region, the depth drops to less than 10.0 ft (3.04 m) and at places reduces to knee deep level during non-monsoon months. With increase of depth following monsoon run-off, the *Hilsa* migration/catch goes up. It is observed that 4.0-4.5 m is favourable depth from surface for migration of adult *Hilsa*.

3.5.4 Migration of Hilsa in the Marine Zone of Hooghly Estuary

Hilsa shad spends most of its life in the inshore areas of the sea and undertakes extensive migrations ascending the estuaries and rivers for breeding (Reuben *et al.*, 1992). The life cycles of most marine and estuarine species involve complex migrations between spawning and nursery grounds. Older *Hilsa* spawn for the second and the third time in the higher reaches, while younger *Hilsa* making their first spawning migration are more susceptible to changes in salinity and spawn in the lower portions of the river (Rahman and Cowx, 2006). Information about larval abundance of species in the northern part of the Bay of Bengal is scarce to identify potential larval grounds.

Identification of actual migratory route requires a long-term study which is beyond the scope of this brief observation. During the eight lunar cycles under study, surveyors could find some indication of migration and subsequent spawning. Maximum aggregation of brood fishes comprising of IVth and Vth stage of maturity was caught at 21°07´81.5´´ N and 88°15´93.1´´ E in commercial fishing during 29th August lunar cycle. Catch data obtained in every lunar cycle during the study period depicted that this aggregation of fishes has gradually shifted towards North-West and reached 21°36´50.0´´ N and 87°56´80.0´´ E (near the confluence of Hooghly river) during 12th October lunar cycle and the school was comprised of good number of female *Hilsa* with Vth and VIth maturity stages. During 26th October lunar cycle, *Hilsa* catch at the confluence of Hooghly river became much less (Figure 3.14). Females caught were mostly in spent condition i.e., in the VIIth or VIIIth stage of maturity. It was thus observed that migration of a school of *Hilsa* took place towards north-west from marine to estuarine, environment and spawning occurred at the confluence of Hooghly river, characterised by lower salinity. Later, the aggregation of brood fishes shifted towards outer estuary. Frequent movement of the schools from east to west and reverse has also been observed which (Figure 3.14) depicted similar aggregation of *Hilsa* during August at the confluence of Hooghly River and little downstream indicating another probable spawning.

Figure 3.13

Depth Variation in the Hooghly-Bhagirathi River System

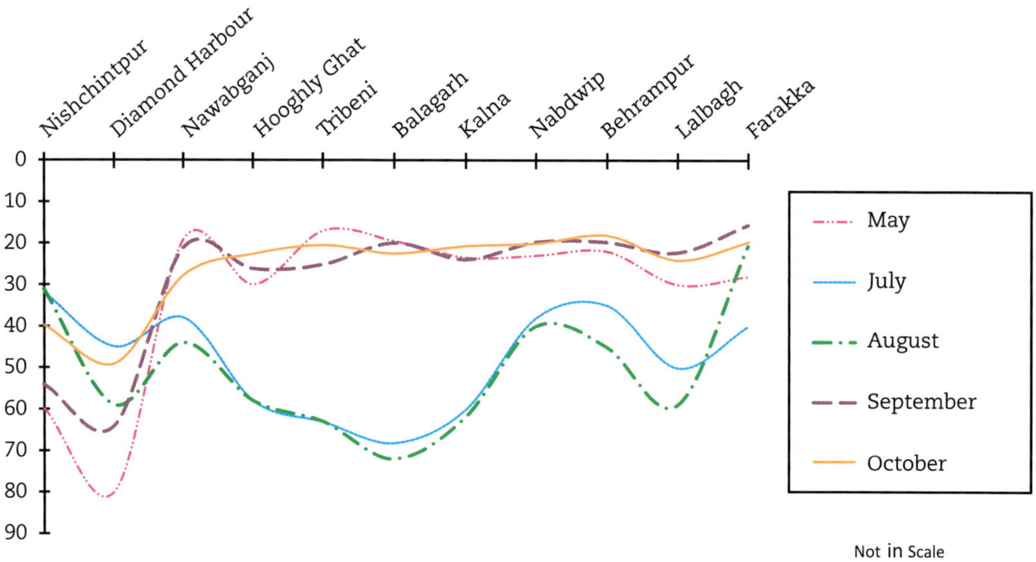

The study of *Hilsa* movement pattern was attempted mainly based on catch data. By using remote sensing and GIS technology, *Hilsa* movement could be understood. The geographical positions of high *Hilsa* catch zone have been put in a geo-referenced image of the Bay of Bengal and attempts have been made to create an output map to understand *Hilsa* migration pattern. During the present study scientists also recognised movement of *Hilsa* stock in the marine and lower estuarine of Hooghly-Matla estuary. It was interesting to observe the shift of major *Hilsa* stock (maximum catch) gradually towards the outer estuary (Figure 3.14) with progression of monsoon.

3.6 Spawning Ground

Hilsa shad spends most of its life in the inshore areas of the sea and undertakes extensive migrations ascending estuaries and rivers for breeding purposes (Reuben *et al.*, 1992). Life cycles of most marine and estuarine species involve complex migrations between spawning and nursery grounds. Older *Hilsa* spawn for the second and third time in the higher reaches, while younger *Hilsa* making their first spawning migration are more susceptible to changes in salinity and spawn in the lower portions of the river (Rahman, 2005).

3.6.1 Spawning Grounds in Bangladesh

Hilsa breeding ground in the Bay of Bengal of Bangladesh is well identified. In Bangladesh, there are four breeding grounds (Table 3.6 and Figure 3.15); however, more studies are recommended to shed light on these breeding grounds and to observe if they are moving in surrounding areas. The spawning ground was detected by availability of brood fish and spent fishes. In the present study, we have taken Bangladesh Fisheries Research Institute (BFRI) and Department of Fisheries (DoF) marked spawning grounds and cross-checked with availability of spent fish during spawning season (see the plate Table 3.6).

3.6.2 Spawning Behaviour in Bhagirathi-Hooghly River System

Research on reproductive biology of *Hilsa* indicated that spawning of this species is seasonal. In almost all major river systems and lagoons *viz.*, Hooghly, Ganga, Chilika, Tapti, Indus, Padma and Meghna, the spawning season of *Hilsa* was noticed during the period between August and October.

The existing knowledge on early growth rate species in the Hooghly estuary as estimated by De (1986; De and Saigal, 1989, De, 2001; Bhaumik *et al.*, 2011) indicated

Figure 3.14

Movement Pattern of *Hilsa* Stock (Maximum Catch) During June-October 2011 in the Outer Hooghly Estuary and the Bay of Bengal

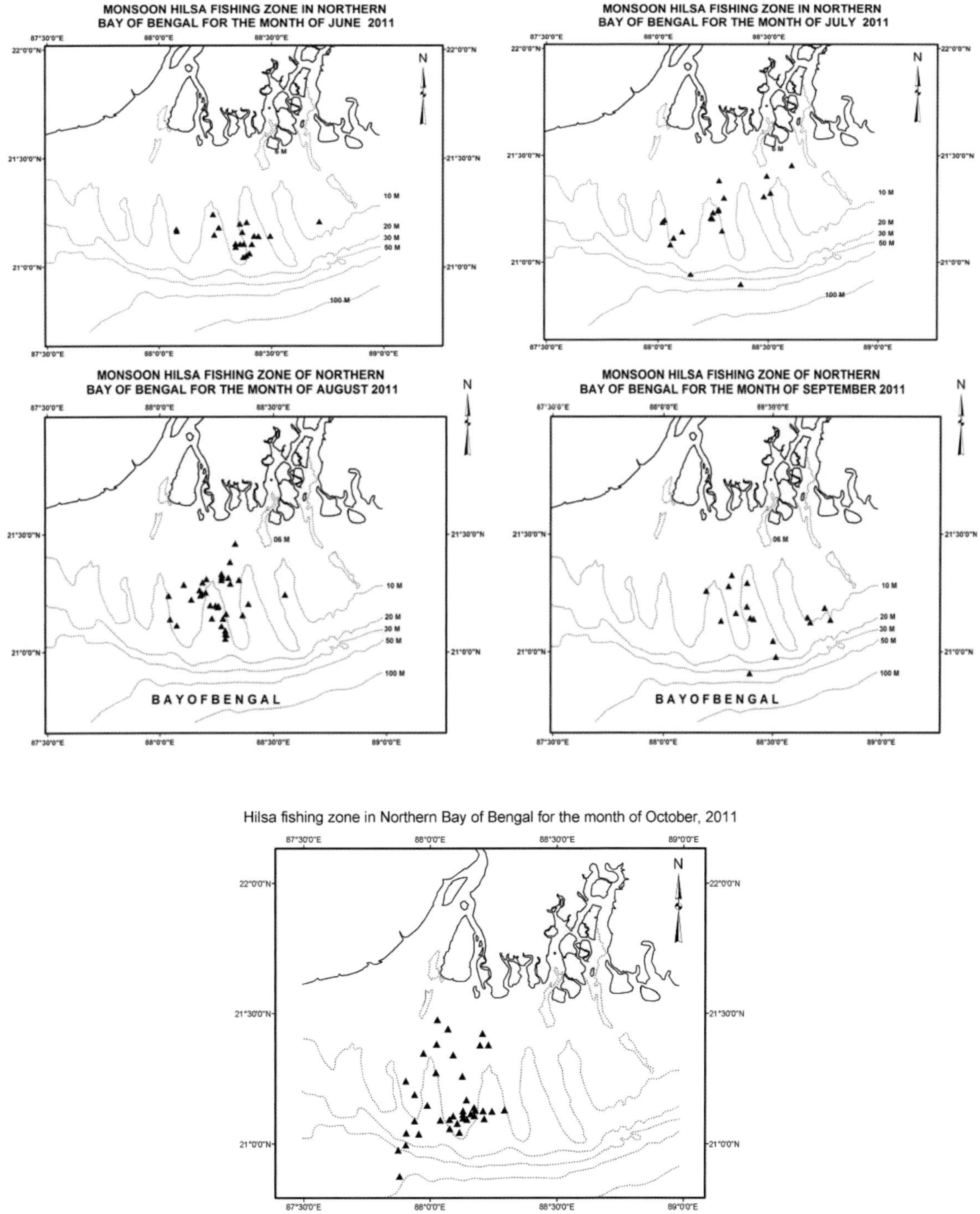

prolonged spawning season of the species i.e., during August-March with peak in October-November and February-March.

Based on this study conducted at the institute in 2011 towards availability of *Hilsa* seed along the entire stretch of the Hooghly-Bhagirathi (Figure 3.17), results indicated that available sizes of juveniles was 40-92 mm in December, 50-90 mm in January, 56-112 mm in February, 70-115 mm in March and 75-149 mm in April. It clearly indicated that major spawning takes place during October–November and minor spawning during May–July and January–March. This was in conformity with the study of Bhanot (1973) who confirmed through collection of *Hilsa* juveniles in the Hooghly estuary that species bred throughout the year with peak activity in February- March, July-August and October-November.

Percentage abundance (Figure 3.16) of the fry (30-40 mm) was considered for demarcating the spawning area. During July-September, two distinct areas between Nishchintpur-Godakhali and Hooghly Ghat-Kalna were observed as the potential breeding zones. In July, the breeding was recorded in the upper freshwater zone (Hooghly Ghat-Kalna) and in August-September the breeding area shifted downstream (Nishchintapur-Godakhali).

During the commencement of the south-west monsoon and consequent flooding of rivers, *Hilsa* starts its spawning migration upstream. A mature *Hilsa* lays eggs; the eggs are deposited in freshwater where hatching takes place in about 23-26 hours at an average temperature of 23°C. The newly hatched larvae were recorded as 2.3 mm in size and the larvae and juveniles made their way downstream to the sea during a period of several months, feeding and growing on the way. At this stage of their life cycle, juveniles of *Hilsa* having the size range of 40-150 mm were widely available during February to May in the foreshore and riverine waters of Hooghly-Bhagirathi river system and other deltic rivers of Sunderbans.

Usually, these juveniles graze from five to six months of age in freshwater before they make a move to sea water. They are caught

Table 3.6

***Hilsa* Shad Breeding Grounds Boundaries in Bangladesh**

Breeding Grounds	*Location*
North Tojumuddin/West Sayed Aulya point	E 90° 49' 12.00", N 22° 19' 56.40"
Shaer Ali/HyetKandi point, Mirsorai	E 91° 28' 55.20", N 22° 42' 57.60"
Lata Chapali point, Kolapara	E 90° 12' 39.60", N 21° 47' 56.40"
North Kutubdya/Gandamara point	E 91° 52' 51.60", N 21° 55' 19.00"

Source: DoF, 2011.

Plate: Spent fish (left two) observed from downstream Chandpur and upstream Laxmipur area (photograph by M.N. Naser).

Figure 3.15

***Hilsa* Breeding Area in Bangladesh**

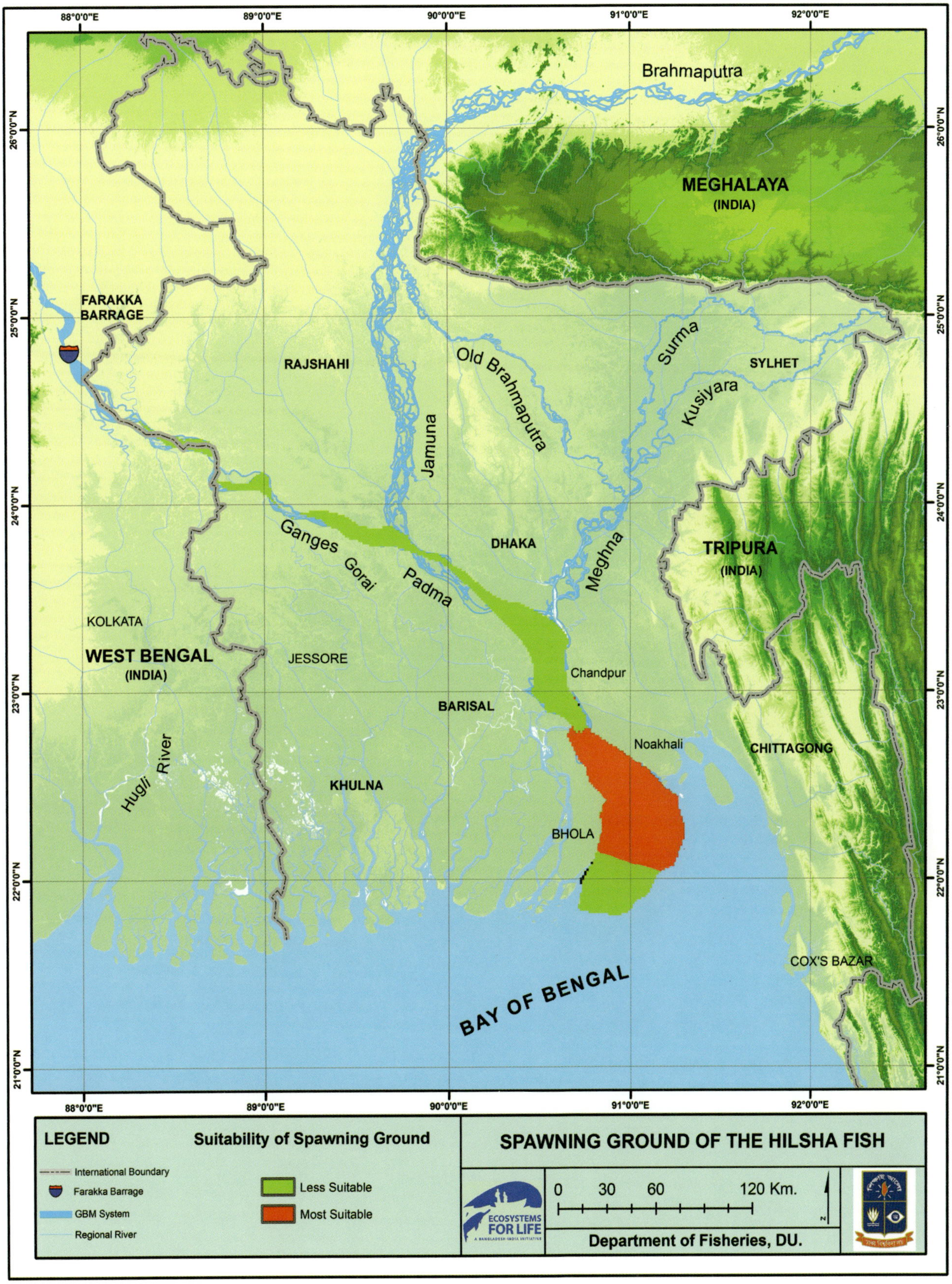

Figure 3.16

Seed Abundance in the Sampling Sites

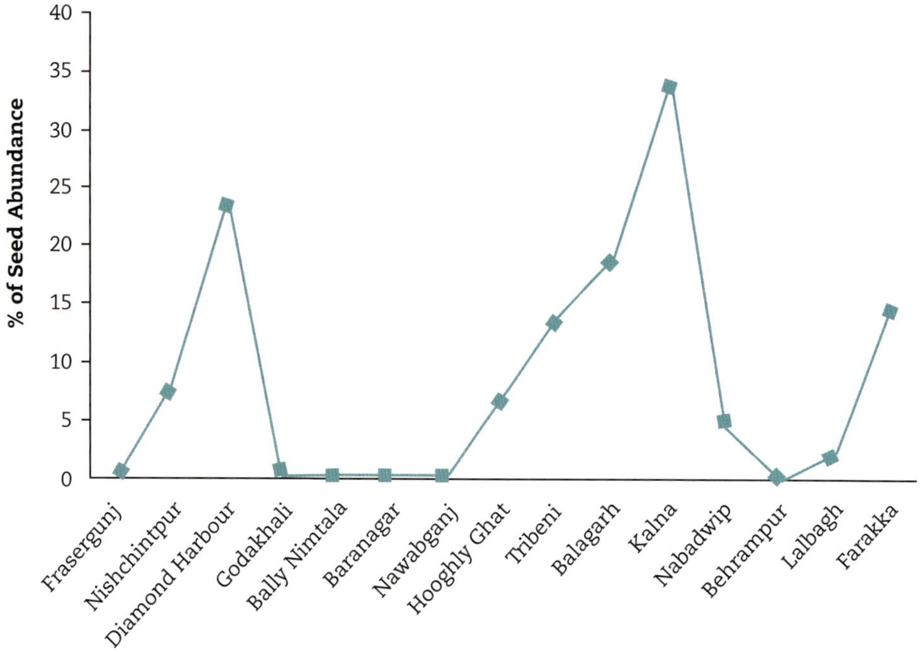

in large numbers using current nets of small mesh size during their grazing period in rivers as well as seashore by artisanal fishermen thus resorting to wanton killing of these tiny fishes.

Stretches between Nishchintpur and Diamond Harbour at downstream, Hooghly Ghat and Kalna in freshwater tidal zone and Lalbagh to Farakka in Bhagirathi river could be demarcated as potential breeding zones for *Hilsa* (Figures 3.17 and 3.19). In 2011, monsoon breeding of *Hilsa* was first observed around Kalna in July. The breeding activities shifted downstream below Diamond Harbour following decreased river discharge and resultant low depth in upper reaches during August and September. Post-monsoon breeding occurred in all demarcated breeding zones with variation in intensity and period.

The combined catch of fry and advanced juveniles was maximum during April and July, 2011. The catch of the advanced juveniles was more downstream between Godakhali and Nishchintpur. The percentage of fry in the total catch was more in the upper freshwater reaches. The presence of advanced juveniles in the entire stretch round the year needs further research.

3.6.3 Recruitment patterns

A mixed population of fry to juveniles (23-163 mm) was available almost round the year with spatio-temporal variability in size and density. The stretch between Nishchintpur and Godakhali produced 34.25 per cent of fry-juveniles. As many as 42.17 per cent of the recruitees were from the upper freshwater tidal zone located between Hooghly Ghat and Kalna. The pattern of recruitment was erratic during post-monsoon season. It was observed that such recruitment was maximum at Farakka region in December 2010. In the period that followed, January and February 2011, the recruitment was higher in upper freshwater tidal zone between Hooghly Ghat and Kalna and comparatively low around Diamond Harbour stretch at the downstream. The advanced juveniles above 100 mm showed a trend of downward movement from April onwards. Early juveniles behaved like resident species of the river-estuarine system and nurtured in comparatively deeper zones, which formed potential areas for their harvest.

Figure 3.17

Tentative Breeding Grounds in the Hooghly-Bhagirathi Stretch

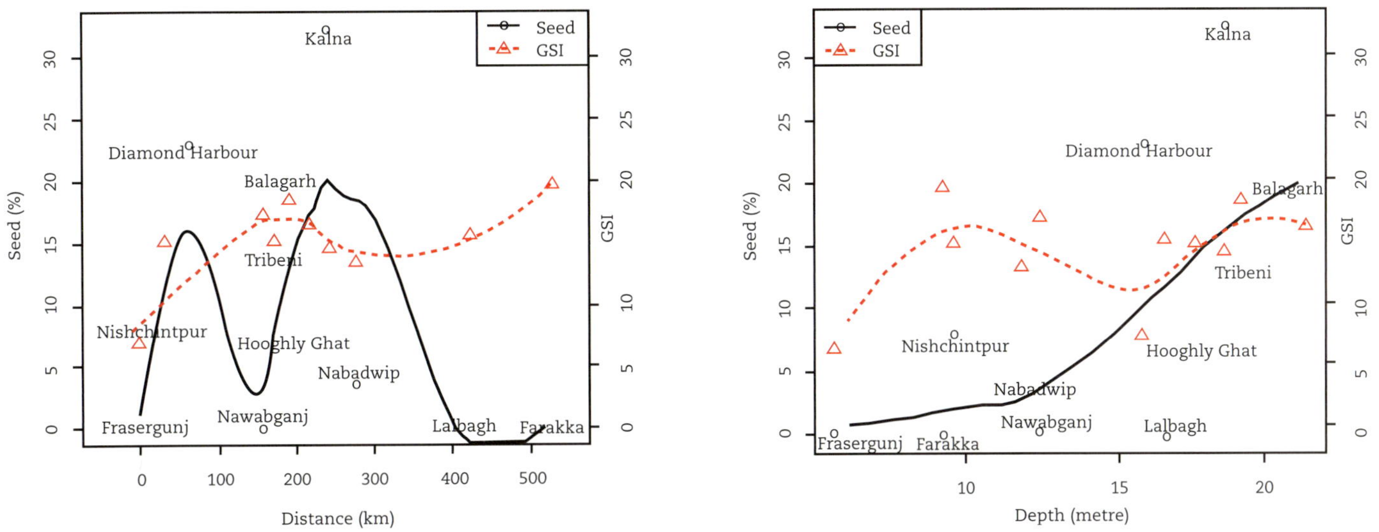

Breeding ground:

1. 50 km distance (around Diamond Harbour).
2. Between 200 km to 300 km distance from sea mouth (Hoogly Ghat to Kalna region).
3. Between 159 km to 71.36 km distance (Lalbagh to Farakka) region.

As depth increases chance of getting seed increases. (Most Favourable river depth for spawnning is 16 metres and above.

Predictive curves were based on lowest smoothing available under R 2.12.2

Figure 3.18

Predictive Map on Seed Availability over Distance from Sea Mouth and River Depth

Shaded green area highly potential breeding zone falling between 200 km to 300km distance from sea mouth

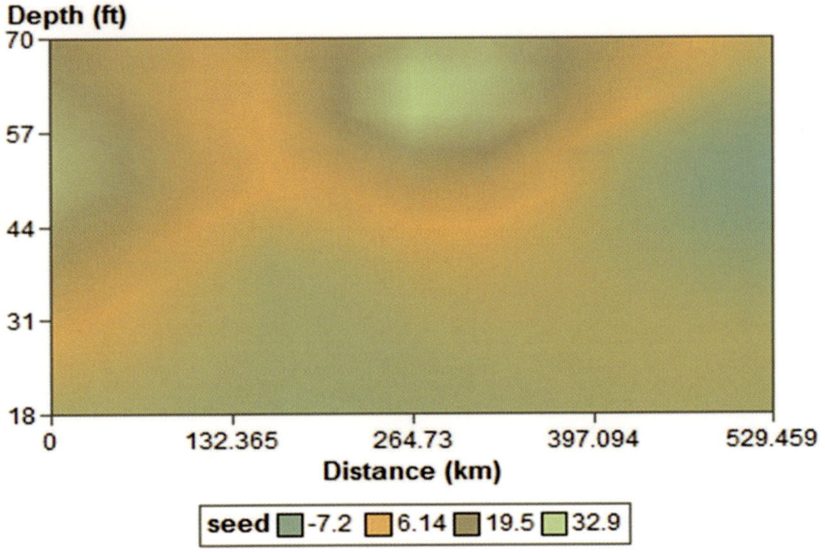

Note: Analysis done by using SAS 9.2, using contour plot with spline smoothing.

Figure 3.19

Satellite Images of Different Zones of the Hooghly-Bhagirathi Stretch

Upper Stretch

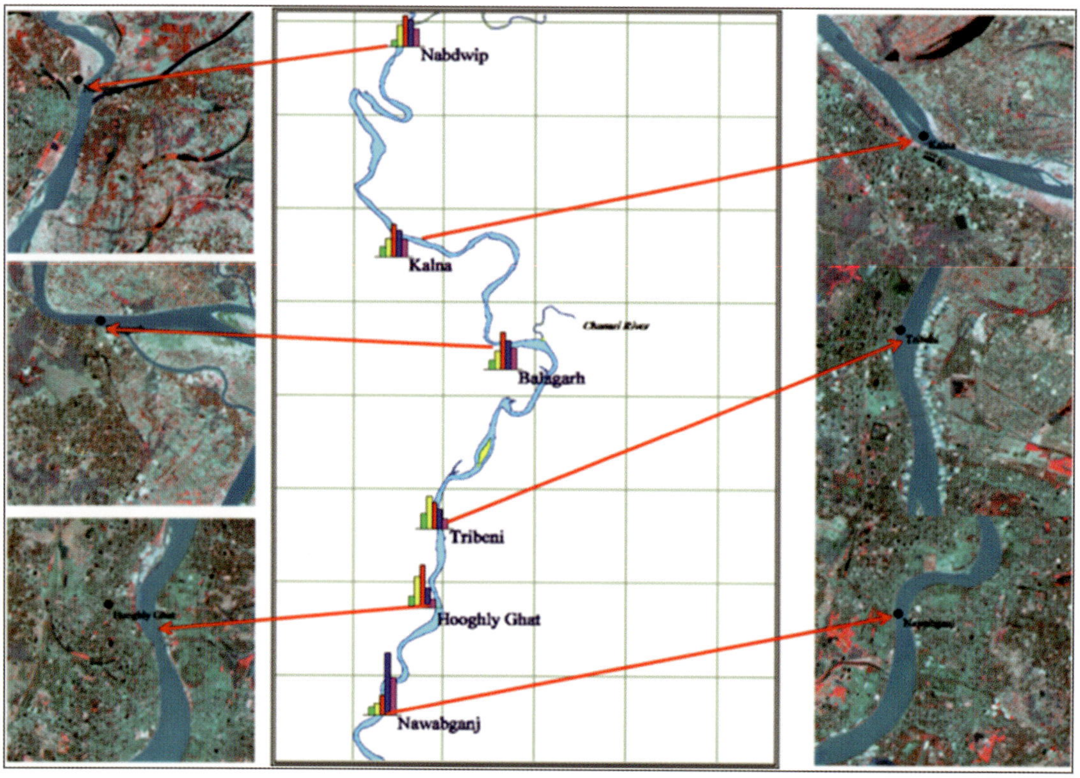

Middle Stretch

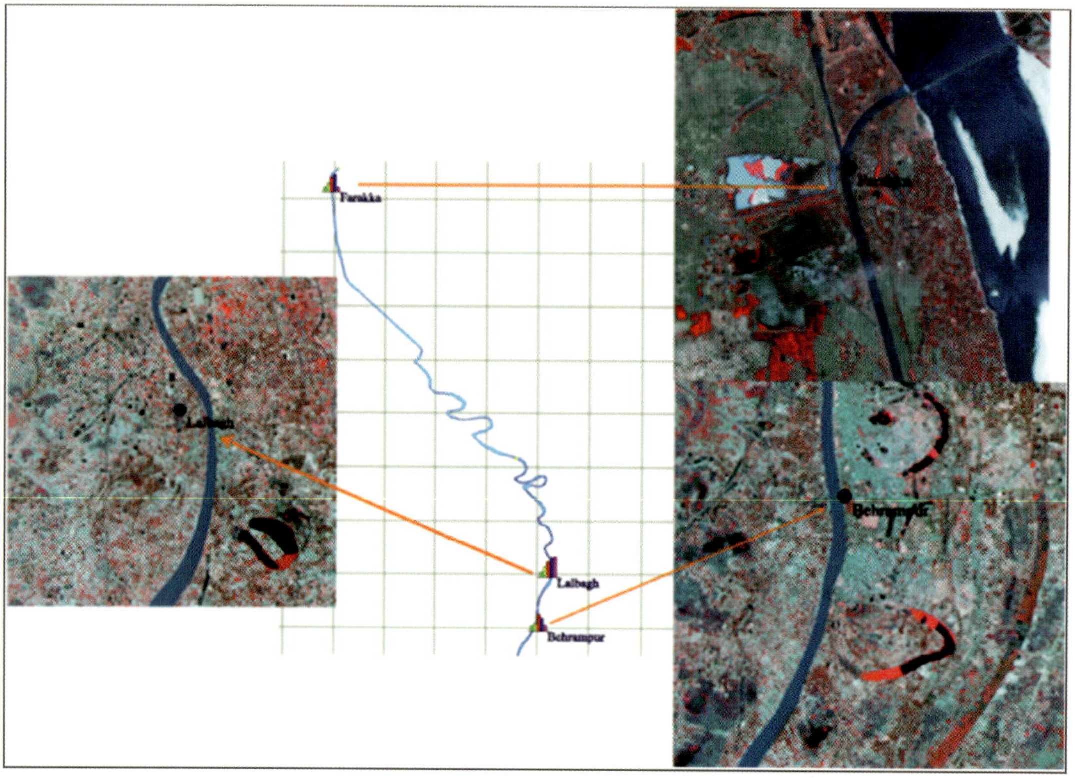

Lower Stretch

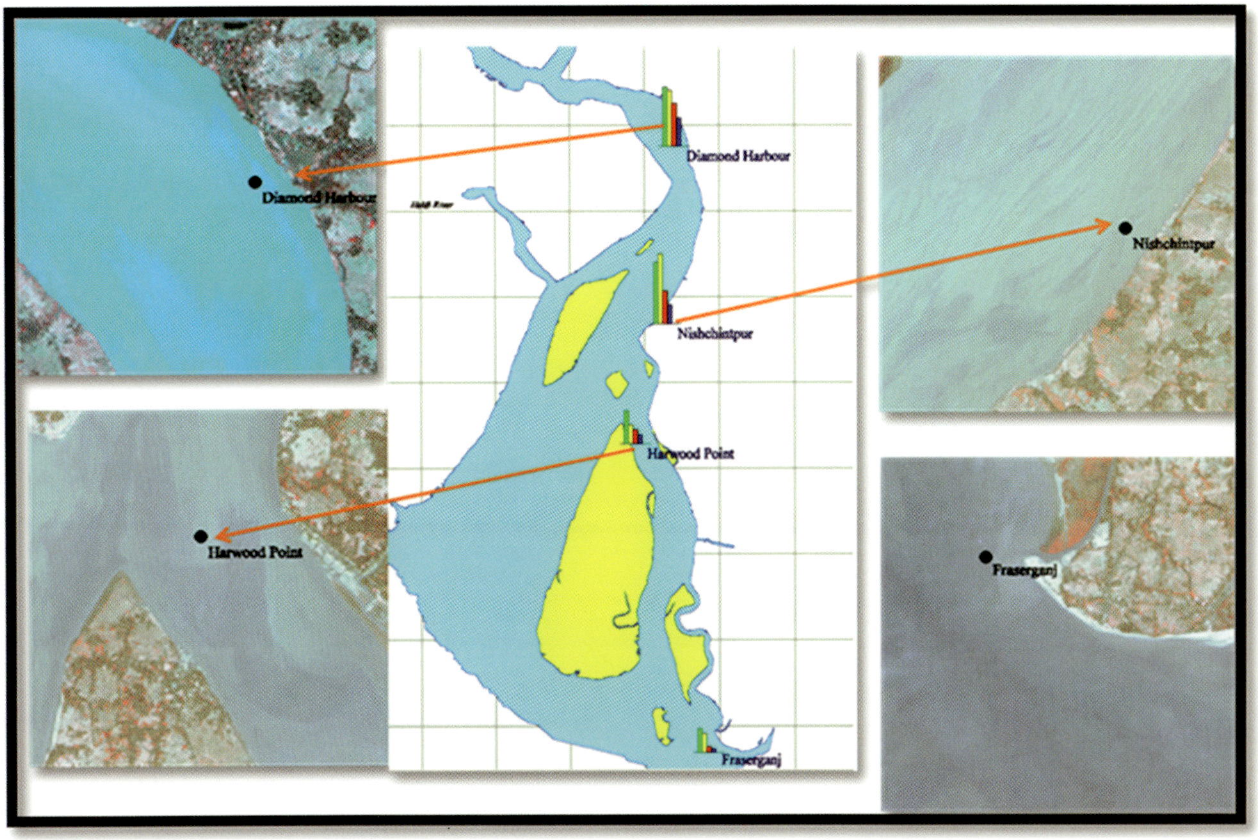

Box 3.1

Breeding Grounds in Hooghly-Bhagirathi System Locate

- Between Diamond Harbour and Godakhali (Lat. 22°10.182'N, Long. 88°12.034'E and Lat. 22°24.284'N, Long. 88°08.548'E),
- Between Hooghly Ghat to Kalna (Lat. 22°25.115'N, Long. 88°23.826'E), and
- Between Lalbagh to Farakka (Lat. 24°05.243'N, Long. 88°27.942'E and Lat. 24°27.253'N, Long. 88°54.470'E)

In the marine and estuarine part, profusion of *Hilsa* juveniles (Table 3.5) was highest in Sagar Island (Station-1) and Frasergunj (Station-2), moderate in Kakdwip (Station-3) and lowest in Canning (Station-4) and Gathkhali (Station-5) samples confirming location of spawning ground at the confluence of Hooghly river. According to a semi-structured interview with fishermen, few other spawning grounds were believed to exist in the lower estuarine area of Matla-Bidya-Raimangal (Ichamti) estuarine complex close to submerged sands of 2-3 meter water depth. Increasing trends in number of *Hilsa* juveniles in Stations 4 and 5 samples indicated possibility of existence of other spawning grounds at the confluence of Matla-Bidya-Raimangal complex. After hatching, the juveniles inferred have been migrated upward for grazing, resulting in increasing numbers. However, this needed to be confirmed by detailed survey and data collection in the estuarine-marine area.

Figure 3.20

Catch per Unit of Effort (CPUE) of Juvenile *Hilsa*

4

Hilsa Shad Fishery Management and Human Interventions

According to Rahman (2001), Bangladesh contributes about 87 per cent of the world *Hilsa* catch (2, 23,177 tonnes), followed by India (7.2%), Pakistan (3.4%), Myanmar (1.3%), Iran (0.3%), Iraq (0.26%) and Kuwait (0.24%). This section reviews the health of *Hilsa* stock as well as the human impediments to *Hilsa* migration and its sustainability in the transboundary ecosystem.

During the last two decades, natural migratory patterns of fishes have been heavily interrupted by construction of dams, barrages, dykes, regulators, fences for flood control and irrigation or fishing purposes, without any provision for the passage of fish (Ghosh, 1987; Kowtal, 1994). Al-Nasiri and Al-Mukhtar (1988) reported that water pollution in Basrah, Iraq, affected the *Hilsa* stocks remarkably. The construction of the Farakka Barrage on the Ganga in 1972 has impacted on *Hilsa* migration and hence its abundance further upstream (Chandra *et al.*, 1987; Jhingran and Gupta, 1987; Mukhopadhyay, 1994; Chandra, 1994; Haldar and Rahman, 1998). The Ukai and Kakrapara dams in Gujarat similarly affected migration of *Hilsa* in the Tapti River of India (Pisolkav, 1994; Dubey, 1994). Due to the construction of obstructions and dams in the Kumar, Nabaganga and Feni rivers in Bangladesh, *Hilsa* fishery in these rivers has been seriously affected (Haldar and Rahman, 1998). Although migration of *Hilsa* is restricted by barrages, it still runs far up the Ganges (*Fish Base*, 2004). Many researchers have identified barriers to *Hilsa* migration as a major factor contributing to the decline of the species (Mazid and Islam, 1991; Rahman, 2001).

4.1 Current Status and Conditions in Bangladesh

The current production of *Hilsa* in Bangladesh was 313,753 metric tonnes in 2009-10. This was 10.82 per cent of the total fish produced in the country. Of this 115,179 metric tonnes of *Hilsa* were caught from inland waters and 198,574 metric tonnes from the Bay of Bengal trawl. With passage of time and development of marine fishing techniques, more *Hilsa* are being caught from the estuarine and marine part of the Bay of Bengal. Even in West Bengal, where the marine catch comprises 70 per cent of the total *Hilsa* catch.

From semi-structured interviews among fishermen, it is revealed that while fishing is the dominant (78%) primary occupation of any fishing village, they mostly earn a monthly income 6,000-8,000 taka and about 61 per cent of them are illiterate. No commercial banks offer any credit facility to these fishermen and they are compelled to sell their fishes to the moneylender at a low price to meet the debt. This is a serious social impediment for developing a sustainable *Hilsa* fishery in the region.

4.2 Impediments to *Hilsa* Migration and Spawning in Bangladesh

The migration of *Hilsa* in Meghna-Padma (Ganges) water system has been hampered by various factors. The low water flow in the Padma river system due to the Farakka barrage in India hampers migration of *Hilsa* towards the Padma river system. The sandy char islands in Padma river systems block the migration route of the *Jatka* fish to former fishing ground of Padma which was the main fishing zone of early 1970s. This situation can be restored by adequate water flow. Use of *ber jal* and *bana* is another hurdle for fish migration. It has been observed that the small water-channel was completely blocked by *ber jal* or *bana* to catch *Hilsa* that enter to the channel during migration time.

The following points emerged as the major impediments of *Hilsa* migration in Bangladesh:

- Over fishing in the estuarine mouth region created barriers and also dispersed *Hilsa* on its way to breeding migration in upper freshwater environment.
- Under-sized fishing through zero and small meshed gill/current nets and unwanted hauling of the juveniles are major human factors affecting the migration, spawning and recruitment success of *Hilsa*.
- Increasing *jatka* fishing by mostly part-time fishermen is a major threat to the sustainability of fish stock. In an interview with fishermen, 80 per cent of the respondents informed that the over-catching of *jatka* is the main reason for the deline of *Hilsa* stock in the rivers of Bangladesh.

- Siltation in river beds due to decreased water flow from upstream (especially during dry season) is one of the major constrains of blockage of migration route of *Hilsa*.
- Regional effort especially in Bangladesh, India and Myanmar is crucial for sustainable *Hilsa* fisheries.

Figure 4.1

Causes of Decline of Fish Availability (Perception of Fishermen)

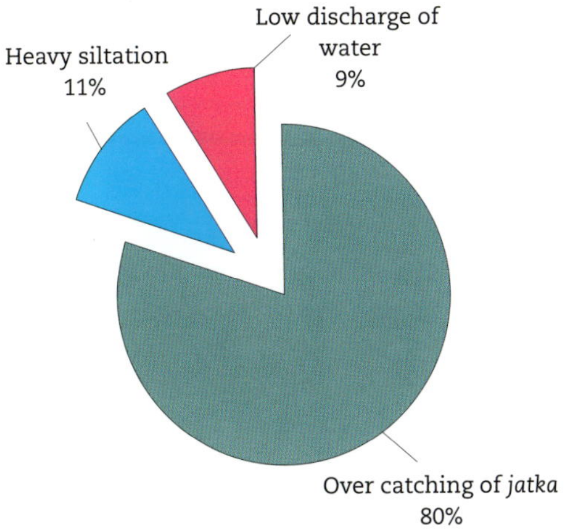

River siltation has been emerged as one of the major problems in Bangladesh. This phenomen leads to a serious threat to river morphology, biodiversity and depended livelihoods as well. The Ganges-Brahamaputra river systems that originated in the Himalyas have generated and provided a huge amount of sediment to the Bay of Bengal. Every year, about 735 million metric tonnes of sediment have been estimated in the river systems (Bangladesh Water Development Board; BWDB). This occurs around the Hatia-Barisal-Patuakhali area where the sediment is up to 18 km thick [Master Plan Organization (MPO), 1986]. In addition to this, it causes quick filling up the river beds by increasing sedimentation, a common scenario in the countries hydrological systems. As a result of future sea-level rise, this increase in sedimentation to the coastal zone may be offset by the 'back water effect', whereby the rise in water level in the Bay of Bengal reduces the ability of rivers to carry sedimentation to the coastal zone (Iqubal and Taha, 2009). The decrease in flow of these river systems due to structural interventions has affected agriculture, fisheries, livestock and both surface and ground water. Due to sedimentation and siltation, there are many adverse impacts to the fish life cycle, particularly for *anadromous* species like the *Hilsa* fish, though they like to migrate in low turbid water with high oxygen level. The major problems are:

- High levels of sedimentation (>200-300 mg/l) can cause fish mortality.
- It reduces sunlight penetration into the water, so it can cause changes fish feeding behaviour.
- Sediments silts can sink or suffocate fish eggs.
- Sediments can carry toxic substances from agriculture and industry that can cause fish death.
- It reduces water transparency that is very crucial for fish spawning and migration as well.
- It narrows and shifts river path that also reason of damaging fish habitat.
- Fishermen also urged that as *Hilsa* is not only considered as a delicious food item but also an integral part of our culture (both in Bangladesh and West Bengal of India) both the government must come forward to conserve the *Hilsa* fishery".

4.3 Human Impact on Spawning and Migration in Hooghly River System

The *Hilsa* fishing activities in Bhagirathi-Hooghly river system mostly concentrate in lower estuarine-marine zone. During peak season of migration of mostly mature fishes, thousands of gill nets are deployed. Over the past two decades, the mesh size of the gill nets *vis-à-vis* the mean size of fish has been reduced remarkably. Further, in migration, the brood stocks face unlimited fishing pressure affecting the breeding success and resultant recruitment of desired natural stock. The post-breeding harvest of *Hilsa* juveniles also has negative impact on the recruitment of natural population of this species.

The following are the major human impediments to *Hilsa* migration in the Hooghly-Bhagirathi river system and estuary.

Box 4.1

Transboundary Action is required for Sustainable *Hilsa* Management

Md Golam Mustafa the President of Charghat (Rajshahi, Bangladesh) Fishermen's Association urged "It's no mean if there is no joint initiative between Bangladesh and India to conserve the *Hilsa* fishery. We stop *Hilsa* harvesting in Padma River during ban period in Bangladesh but India has no ban period. So, on the other bank of the Padma river (which is known as Ganga in Indian part) the Indian fishermen continue harvesting round the year even during the breeding period. Bangladesh and India share the common stock of *Hilsa*, so, without the joint ban period and measures we cannot think about the sustainable *Hilsa* fishery."

4.3.1 Siltation in Estuary Mouth

Catchment modification and resultant carriage of soil particle to the river course has remarkably elevated the bed level. The mouth of the estuary is gradually affected by siltation creating serious hindrance for *Hilsa* migration into the estuarine system.

4.3.2 Impact of Barrages, Dams, etc.

Construction of dams, barrages, anicuts, etc., over the rivers has created an obstruction in migration of *Hilsa* resulting in sharp decline of its fisheries at upper reaches. The barrages or dams also deprive water flow requirement for spawning and migration of *Hilsa*. As per earlier reports, *Hilsa* use to migrate even up to Delhi through river Ganga and similarly it was also recorded from Agra and Kanpur. After commissioning of Farakka barrage over the river Ganga in 1975, *Hilsa* fisheries at upstream of the barrage was negligible in most of the fish landing centres. Eventually an average of 92 per cent reduction in *Hilsa* catch at upstream of Farakka barrage was estimated by the Central Inland Fisheries Research Institute (CIFRI) due to construction of the barrage. Even at Allahabad, where *Hilsa* used to occupy a significant share in total fish catch, shares only a meager percentage of the harvest.

4.3.3 Juvenile Fishing

Hilsa breeds through a prolonged breeding season as evidenced by availability of *Hilsa* seed from August to May. This suggests that spawning is not simultaneous for all ascending individuals. Traditionally *Hilsa* juveniles are often caught in small-mesh bag net, small-mesh gill net, shooting net, seine net, drag net and scoop net during their migration towards sea especially during November to May and sometimes extending up to July in the river. The recent investigation in 2010 recorded a very alarming situation when a single bag net catch of 10 kg at Godakhali near Budge Budge had a share of 2.8 kg very small *Hilsa* juveniles at 5-20 g weight. Similarly, the catch of scoop nets (locally called *vetijal*) operated between Sodepur and Budge during March consisted mostly of *Hilsa* juveniles (>90% by numbers in total fish caught).

The estimated catch of these juveniles fluctuated between 41.1 tonnes and 151.01 tonnes with an average of 85 tonnes per year during 1998-2010. Their size ranged between 62 mm and 155 mm in length and 2-28 g in weight. An extrapolated estimation reveals that 50 per cent reduction of the juvenile *Hilsa* killing has the potentiality to increase the adult production by about 10 per cent. Another estimate reports that if even 1 per cent more *Hilsha* juvenile could be saved, then the production of adult *Hilsa* could be increased by 4000 tonnes/year.

4.3.4 Exploitation of Brood Fishes

The fishermen capture gravid female *Hilsa* during their upstream breeding migration mostly at estuary mouth during monsoon. This has a tremendous adverse impact on population recruitment and declining of *Hilsa* fisheries. The undersised *Hilsa* (below 500 g) are being caught in huge numbers using monofilament nets at Frazerganj-Namkhana area in Hooghly estuary defeating the very cause of stock sustenance and leading to decline in of *Hilsa* fishery of the Bhagirathi-Hooghly riverine system. Fish catch recorded from five mechanised boats at the Frazerganj fishing harbour was 5.6 tonnes out of which *Hilsa* alone was 3.2 tonnes (56.3%) and 66 per cent of them were female fish. The observations on maturity conditions revealed that 59.8 per cent of the fishes were in 4th stage of maturity followed by 26.3 per cent in 3rd stage, 7.5 per cent in 2nd stage and 6.4 per cent in 5th stage.

4.3.5 Lack of Mesh Size Regulation

Presently fishing with small mesh sized (<60 mm) gill nets are mainly responsible for reducing the size of *Hilsa* in the coastal region as well as in the freshwaters of the Bhagirathi-Hooghly riverine system.

4.3.6 Over-Fishing

The trend of fish catch in the Bhagirathi-Hooghly riverine system indicated significant increase during the post-Farakka Barrage period, primarily due to manifold increase in *Hilsa* catch. In recent years, between 1998-99 and 2002-03, the average annual catch of *Hilsa* in the riverine part has been estimated at 11,482.9 tonnes with an impressive increase of 63.3 per cent from the corresponding five years (6279.6 tonnes). Over the years, however, the mean

Figure 4.2

***Hilsa* Sale from Diamond Harbour Market in 2009-2011**

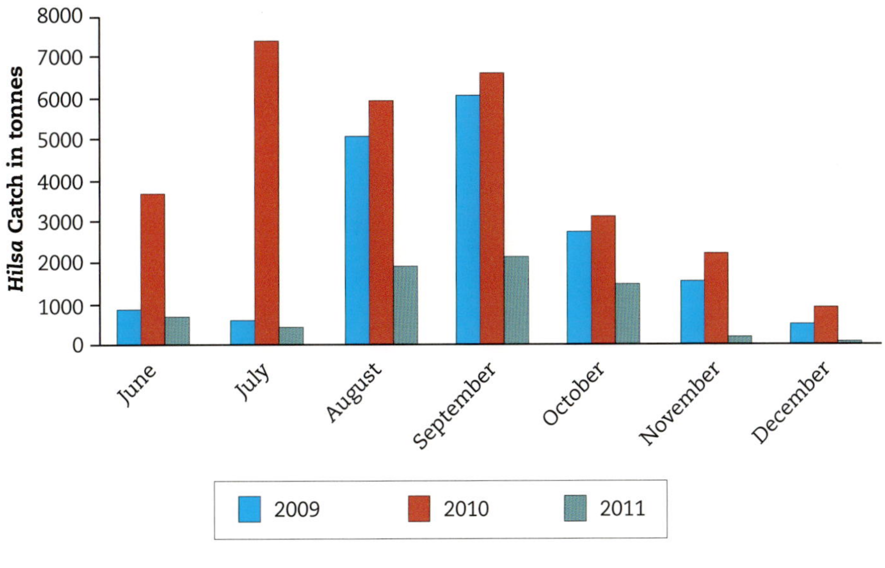

Figure 4.3

Month-wise Catch per Unit Effort (CPUE) in West Bengal Coast, 2011

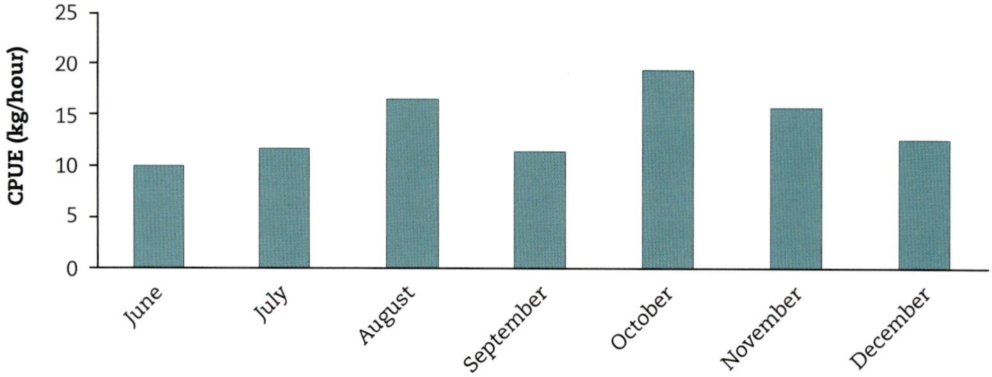

length of *Hilsa* has declined, from 356 mm (1960s) to 300 mm or even less (2000s)—a manifestation of increased efforts, indicating over-fishing.

To understand the stresses on the *Hilsa* stock, the total *Hilsa* catch of Sundarban area has been analysed (figure 4.2) from the market sales data of Diamond Harbour fish market for three years. Though in 2011, the *Hilsa* catch (stock) is extremely poor, probably due to a breeding failure in 2010, there appears to be a yearly variability depending upon rainfall in the early monsoon. The catch dynamics needs a longer multivariant assessment correlating the catch with effort, monsoon rainfall, cyclonic depressions, temperature, salinity, wind speed and direction and other biophysical parameters of the river and the ocean.

In the absence of information about exact number of boats (mechanised, non-mechanised and trawlers) operative at present in the lower estuarine to marine area and their catch details, the catch per haul (effort, kg of *Hilsa*/Hour) data of some control mechanised boat using gill net in the lower estuary have been used. It is observed that during October 2011 catch per unit effort (CPUE) has been highest (19.32±22.1) whereas it was low during June (10.05±7.92) and July (11.64±18.95). The CPUE increases in August (16.45±16.86) and reduced in September (11.53±11.34) and picks up to again the previous level during October. The CPUE decreases in November (15.67±8.73) and December (12.65±6.09).

Another attempt has been made to estimate the CPUE per boat from the fish landing data of Frazergunj fishing harbor at Sundarban. A 10 year data of fish landing *vis à vis* number of registered boats shows that with 90 per cent increase in number of boats the catch of *Hilsa* has increased by 230 per cent. This is also related to increasing level of technology adaptation and capacity building in the marine fishing sector. However, it also indicates that though the CPUE has steadily increased from 13 to 33 up to 2007, it has dipped to 23 in 2010 in spite of a record harvest which indicates that the *Hilsa* fishing has crossed is sustainable yield limit due to overfishing after 2007.

4.3.7 Ineffective Fish Pass

Fish pass provided in Farakka barrage is non-functional at the present point of time. Tagging experiments conducted by CIFRI revealed that *Hilsa* from Bhagirathi-Hooghly riverine system cannot move across the barrage due to obstruction of the three tire sluice gates. However, *Hilsa* can negotiate and pass through Farakka barrage to a small extent during monsoon from Padma side when all gates are opened.

4.3.8 Loss of Habitat

Increased water abstraction for irrigation as well as use for industrial purpose resulted in reduction of water volume in parts of upper Hooghly estuary which has caused loss of breeding and spawning habitats. Siltation in rivers reduced the water depth unsuitable for *Hilsa* migration. It was observed that *Hilsa* prefers migration at a depth 4-5 m. The loss in habitat is directly related to the recruitment potential of *Hilsa* fishery.

4.3.9 Pollution

Ecological aberrations due to industrial and domestic effluents noticed in selective zones and periodically in most of the river systems also inhibit the upstream migration. Hooghly-Matlah estuarine system flows through highly industrialised area like Haldia complex and Kolkata-Howrah metropolis and receives domestic refuse from thickly populated city areas, and effluent from industrial establishments. This exerts great stress to migratory fishes like *Hilsa*.

4.4 Towards a Policy for Sustainable *Hilsa* Fishery Management

4.4.1 Hilsa Conservation Programme in Bangladesh

The Bangladesh government has undertaken an extensive *Hilsa* management action plan. The Government is trying to increase *Hilsa* production not only by conserving *jatka* but also protecting the brood *Hilsa* during the breeding seasons.

4.4.2 Implementation of Jatka Protection Programme

The government of Bangladesh has adopted a programme to protect *jatka* in 2003-04 to ensure sustainable *Hilsa* production. By this programme, *jatka* catch, sell, carry and transport has been prohibited during 1st November to 31st May (7 months). Through participation of all concerned, this *jatka* protection programme is being implemented and already there had been a positive impact on *Hilsa* production in last 8 years. Through successful implementation of the *jatka* protection programme, annual *Hilsa* production has gradually increased in recent years. For the sustainable *Hilsa* production, the government has taken different management steps besides the *jatka* protection programme. In continuity of this success, detailed and strengthened programmes have been adopted and implemented in 2007-08 by different programmes and projects. Government observed "*Jatka* Conservation Week" during 4th to 10th April, 2011.

Based on the experience of execution of the *jatka* protection programme of the last few years, an action plan for smooth execution of the programme for 2008-09 was adopted in October 2008. This action plan specified the activities to protect *jatka*, developed the implementation strategy, ascertained responsibility of relevant agencies and target community and fixed specific timeframe for implementation. This action plan has been implemented in 91 *upazilas* of 20 districts.

4.4.3 Management of Hilsa Sanctuaries

Four sites have been declared as *Hilsa* sanctuaries under the Protection and Conservation of Fish Act 1950 to achieve desired level of protection of *Hilsa*. Apart from these four, another sanctuary has been established at lower Padma in Saritpur district in this year (Table 4.1). In the following five *Hilsa* sanctuaries, all types of fish catch have been banned during certain periods of time every year.

4.4.4 Conservation and Management Measures for Hilsa

Department of Fisheries (DoF), Bangladesh, has approved numerous management measures to escalate *Hilsa* production as well as to sustain the *Hilsa* stock in nature. Amongst all the management measures, the most significant initiatives which have been undertaken by DoF were the conservation of *jatka* (young *Hilsa*) through declaring four *Hilsa* sanctuaries in major nursery grounds and spawning grounds of river system (Table 4.1) and protection of gravid *Hilsa* catches for 10 days during the peak spawning season no fishing in spawning (Table 4.2).

From 2011, new management strategies have been undertaken by DoF (Table 4.3).

Catching of all kind of *Hilsa* fishes, carry, transport, offer, sell, export or possessing throughout the country along with the *Hilsa* spawning grounds mentioned in Tables 3.6 are prohibited for 5 days before and 5 days after the full moon, including the day of full moon, that is total 11 (eleven) days of the moon which first appears in Bengali month of *Aswin* (October) each year.

It is not unlikely that *jatka* fishers earn their livelihood by selling *jatka* and they do

Table 4.1

Hilsa Sanctuary in Bangladesh

Sl No.	Sanctuary Area	Ban Period
1.	From Shatnol of Chandpur district to Char Alexander of Laxmipur (100 km of lower Meghna estuary)	March to April
2.	Madanpur/Char *Hilsa* to Char Pial in Bhola district (90 km area of Shahbajpur river, a tributary of Meghna)	March to April
3.	Bheduria of Bhola district to Char Rustam of Patuakhali district (nearly 100 km of Tetulia river)	March to April
4.	Whole 40 km stretch of Andharmanik river in Patuakhali district	November to January
5.	20 km stretch of Lower Padma River between Shariatpur in the north and chandpur and Shariatpur in the south	March to April

Source: DoF, 2011.

Table 4.2

No _Hilsa_ Catch Zone and Peak Spawning Period of _Hilsa_

Position	Area	Peak Spawning Period (Ban Period of Hilsa catch)
North-East	Shaher Khali/Haithkandi point, Mirersharai	15-24 October
North-West	North Tajumuddin/West Syed Awlia point	15-24 October
South-East	North Kutubdia/Gandamara point	15-24 October
South-West	Lata Chapili point/Kalapara	15-24 October

Source: DoF, 2011.

Table 4.3

Hilsa Sanctuaries in Lower Padma River

Hilsa Fish Sanctuary Area	Ban Period
Lower Meghna (Chandpur-Laxmipur)	March to April (mid *Falgun* to mid *Baishak**)
Shahbazpur Channel (Bhola)	March to April (mid *Falgun* to mid *Baishak**)
Tentulia River (Bhola)	March to April (mid *Falgun* to mid *Baishak**)
Lower Padma river (Shariatpur)	March to April (mid *Falgun* to mid *Baishak**)
Andermanik River (Patuakhali)	November to January (mid *Kartik* to mid *Magh**)

Source: Rahman *et al.* 2011 * Bengali month.

not have any alternate source of income. That's why the government has given special importance this year for alternate sources of income for *jatka* fishermen so that they can earn their livelihoods by some other means during the 'no catch period' of *jatka*. For the rehabilitation of *jatka* fishers there was a programme named '*Jatka* Protection and Jatka Fishers Rehabilitation Programe'. A total of Tk.2.00 crores/year has been allocated for rehabilitation of *jatka* fishermen during the years 2008-2010. Beside this programme a project named "Jatka Conservation, Alternate Income Generation for the *Jatka* Fishers and Research Project" has been implemented within *jatka* available and sanctuary surrounding *upazilas* for giving alternate income generation activities during the ban period. As this rehabilitation

Figure 4.4

Rehabilitation and Alternative Income Generating Activities for *Jatka* Fishers

***Hilsa* Shad Sanctuaries in Bangladesh**

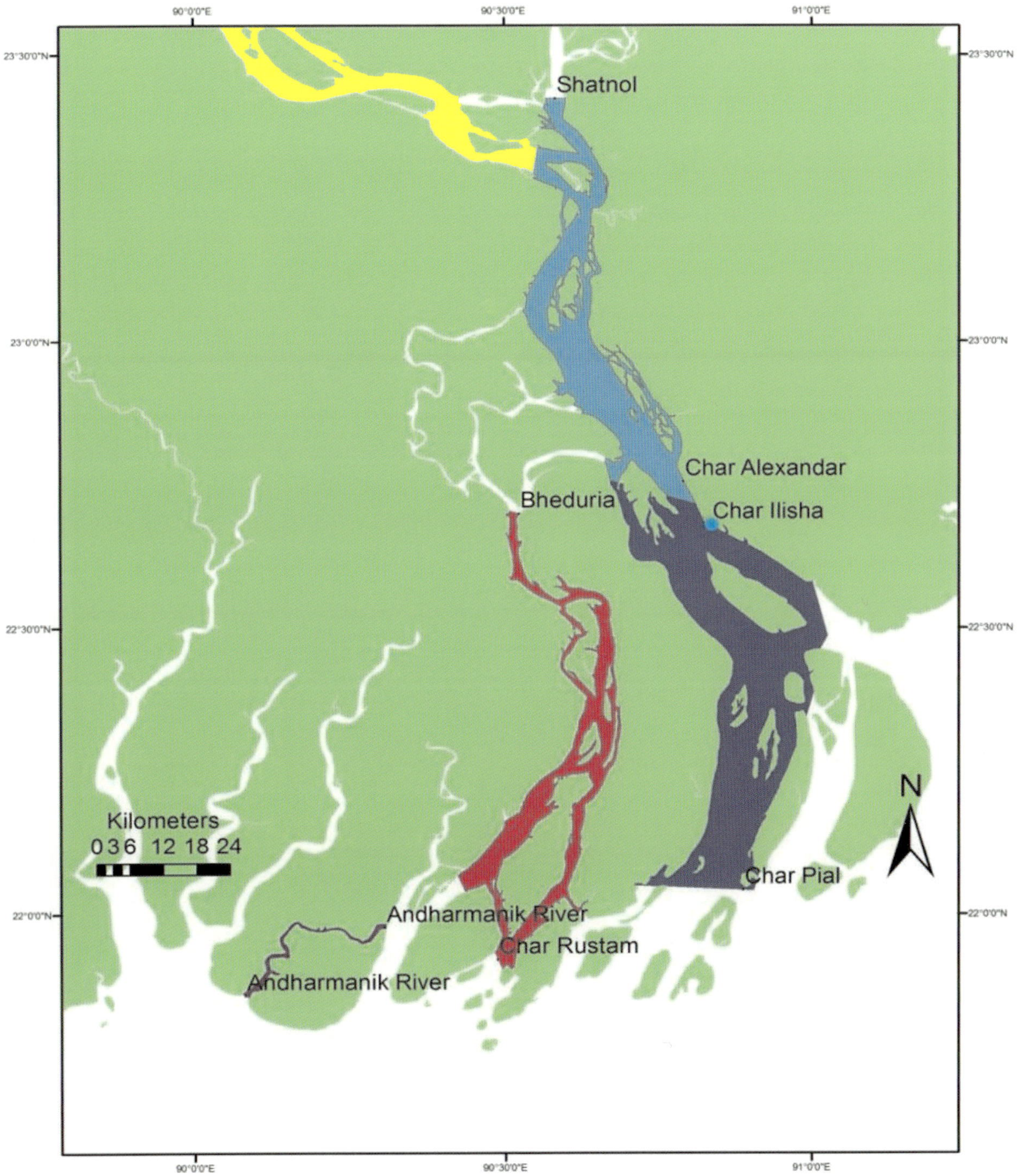

programme was implemented and it helped their livelihood, this made it comparatively easy to keep the fishermen away from catching *jatka*. This project covers 21 *upazilas* of 4 districts. Through this project the Government has allocated 10,000 Tk for each *jatka* fisheries to maintain their family during the *jatka* catch ban period since the project started.

4.5 *Hilsa* Spawning Ground Protection

Every year during the full moon of the Bengali month of *Aswin* (5-16 October in 2011) for 11 days, catch of *Hilsa* is banned in all major spawning ground, the area which is about 7,000 sq km. The law is being revised in 2012, according to which 5 days before and 5 days after the full moon, including the day of full moon, that is 11 days of the full moon which will be first appeared in the Bengali month of *Aswin* each year. Different awareness programmes have been conducted such as poster and leaflet distribution, meeting, rally, dramas, advertisement in radio and TV during the peak spawning period in the concerned areas. Intensive law enforcement activities have been implemented in the *Hilsa* spawning ground on that particular period.

4.6. VGF Programme for *Hilsa* Fishermen

The Government initiated to help the fishers affected by *Hilsa* ban which includes rice provision through VGF (vulnerable group feeding) per household for four months during the ban period in order to mitigate the sufferings of the fishermen. This programme has started since 2004-05. Programme has covered 85 *upazilas* of 15 districts for each year.

4.7 New Heads of Accounts for *Jatka* and Brood *Hilsa* Protection and Conservation

Two new financial codes have been created for *Hilsa* protection in national budget. Taka 2.0 crore was allocated in 2008-09 to conduct *jatka* protection under 3-4401-0001-6605 special operation code and another 2.0 crore under rehabilitation for *jatka* catching fishermen 3-4496-4814-6602.

4.8 Agencies involved in Protection Programme

- Ministry of Fisheries and Livestock, Bangladesh
- Department of Fisheries,
- Bangladesh Fisheries Research Institute
- Bangladesh Navy
- Fisheries and Livestock Information Department (FLID)
- Bangladesh Coast Guard
- District and *upazila* administration
- District and *upazila* Police & Rapid Action Battalion (RAB)
- District and *upazila* level offices of Department of Fisheries

4.9 *Hilsa* Conservation Programme in India

This study observes that there is no *Hilsa* conservation programme in India though India contributes 7.2 per cent of the world *Hilsa* catch.

In order to save the *Hilsa* for sustainable fishery in Hooghly-Bhagirathi river system in India, it is the right time to develop a rational conservation strategy. Mono-filamentous fishing gears possessing mesh size of 80-85 mm or even less are being used to exploit undersised *Hilsa* of less than 500 g in proximity to mouth of Hooghly estuary. This denies the fish to breed and the very purpose of developing sustainable *Hilsa* fisheries is greatly defeated (Bhaumik *et al.*, 2011). Observations in the fish catch of a few mechanised boats operating from Frazerganj fishing harbour revealed that *Hilsa* contributed 56.3 per cent of total catch of 3.2 tonnes and most of the fishes (66%) were female where 59.8 per cent of fish have been observed to be attaining 4th stage of maturity. A concern for bottom trawling by foreign vessels has also been raised, besides exploiting *Hilsa*, they are also ruining the breeding grounds of a number of fin and shell fish. Bag net fishing is rampant and this is denying the *Hilsa* juveniles to contribute towards fisheries. There is practically no control on fishing efforts and compliance of observing closed season is limited and there is hardly any gear restrictions due to open access, lack of social awareness, poor control and surveillance.

Box 4.2

- Migration of *Hilsa* in Hooghly-Bhagirathi system observed to be related with the amplitude of flood and depth profile of the estuarine-river course.
- Spawning of the species dependent on factors like the maturity condition (gonado-somatic index; GST), river hydrography and hydrology and meteorological parameters.
- Intensive fishing in the estuarine mouth region created barrier and also dispersed *Hilsa* on the way to breeding migration in upper freshwater environment.
- Undersized fishing through small meshed gill nets and unwanted hauling of the juveniles observed as major human factors affecting the migration, spawning and recruitment success of *Hilsa*.
- An immediate need to formulate effective measures and also bye-laws to protect precious breeders and potential breeding grounds.

4.9.1 *Desired Measures towards Responsible Fishery*

Technical measures for effecting improvisation in harvesting methods and employing conservational measures are the main concerns at state as well as at central level. An official fishing ban in marine fisheries sector exists from 15th April to 15th June in West Bengal which does not coincide with the period when migration of brood fishes takes place. There is a need to enforce the laws in a more realistic manner. Fine meshed gears (*meen jaal*) are employed which are non-selective and cause comprehensive loss due to non-compliance of Code of Conduct of Responsible Fisheries (CCRF).

4.9.2 *Monitoring, Control and Surveillance (MCS)*

Monitoring, control and surveillance on the fisheries are important aspects to be implemented for sustainable *Hilsa* fishery in the Hooghly-Bhagirathi river system. Presently, there is hardly any control over the exploitation systems being practised by fishers in the estuary. This is like an open access to everyone, although licensing codes imposed by the State Government exists. There seems to be inadequate resource management policies where the enforcement agency expresses their helplessness due to limited man power and other infrastructure facilities. The fishers and other user groups find it very difficult to comply with the rules and regulations due to their poor socioeconomic status. As such, the surveillance towards responsible fishing is very poor resulting in destructive fishing not only by the fishers of the national arena but also by the foreign intruders.

4.9.3 *Possible Modification of Management Protocols*

Possible modifications in prevailing management practices may be exercised by bringing in holistic ecosystem based approaches of management since institutional management arrangements vested with various stakeholders do not adequately address the challenges, which the *Hilsa* fishery faces today. A score of factors *viz.* overexploitation, negative habitat modifications, climate change, etc., have contributed to the decline of *Hilsa* fisheries but it is the high time to render due impetus to human activities overridingly effecting the management of *Hilsa* fisheries. Habitat improvement following stock assessment, harvest management decisions including closed season declaration, closed area provision and ban on negative fishing methods and a strong monitoring machinery are urgently needed.

5

Policy Recommendations

The study was completed in November 2011 and has been finalised following a peer review process. It has come up with a set of policy options that could be adopted in both the countries through advocacy to the involved policy makers. An important aim of Ecosystems for Life is to contribute sustainable and viable options to the development of policies related to natural resources management. Next to the scientific research input this crucially requires thorough consultation of stakeholders. During various consultations, it has been the suggestion of stakeholders—including the research community, conservationists and representatives from fishing associations—that the research findings and recommendations should be tabled at a larger gathering of people from both the countries to devise an effective strategy for *Hilsa* conservation supported by both policy and grass-roots levels. Moreover Project Advisory Committee (PAC), comprising eminent persons from Bangladesh and India, has also emphasised the need for such a comprehensive dialogue as a crucial next step to take the research towards policy development and implementation. This has been strongly support by Central Inland Fisheries Research Institute (CIFRI), India, member of the joint research team (JRT) and co-sponsor of this Dialogue Meeting. It is also important to take follow-up action on the *Hilsa* report as recommended to introduce in West Bengal the steps similar to those taken in Bangladesh for *Hilsa* conservation.

The study and related stakeholder consultations have produced a set of policy options that could be adopted in both the countries and included in policy formulation on conservation of the species. Those were distinguished for the two countries, Bangladesh and India, in addition to recommendations for joint action. These were shared and discussed in the Transboundary Policy Dialogue on *Hilsa* Fisheries Management held on 24 July 2012 at Indi Smart Hotel, Salt Lake, Kolkata, India. The State Minister Fisheries, Department of Fisheries (DoF), Government of West Bengal and two Members of the Parliamentary Standing Committee for the Ministry of Fisheries and Livestock, Government of Bangladesh were present on the occasion. The dialogue which brought together scientists, policy makers and representatives of fishing communities from Bangladesh and India, yielded a set of recommendations. The recommendations were discussed in a meeting between Mr Tarun Shridhar, Joint Secretary (Fisheries), Government of India, and his counterpart from Bangladesh, Mr M. Shamsul Kibria, on 26 July in Kolkata. The International Union for Conservation of Nature (IUCN) Country Representatives of India and Bangladesh Country Office, Ms Meenakshi Datta Ghosh and Mr Ishtiaq Uddin Ahmad and other project staff were also present at the discussion. The meeting discussed the policy options which were presented in the policy dialogue on *Hilsa* conservation. The recommendations were also discussed in the Parliamentary Standing Committee Meeting held on 12 August in Dhaka.

5.1 Policy Recommendations

5.1.1 For Bangladesh

- Management and monitoring systems are essential to ensure effective implementation for existing policies of banning fishing and subsidy distribution. The option to provide fiscal subsidies instead of gratis food support during the *Hilsa* fishing ban period may be considered at an appropriate level.

- It is important to involve all stakeholders in monitoring and policy implementation programmes. Bottom-up approaches should be taken to improve monitoring and implementation frameworks and for finalization of beneficiaries lists under *Hilsa* management programmes.

- To build awareness of *jatka*[1] conservation and sustainable *Hilsa* management print and electronic media should be used. During the breeding season, mass media can be used to broadcast regular features on *Hilsa*. This will allow

1. Immature *Hilsa* fish (6-10 cm) at their juvenile stage of life cycle are known as *jatka*. *Source*: Banglapedia, 2006.

fishermen, local people and *Hilsa* consumers to become aware of the importance of *Hilsa* fishery conservation and assist with the sustainable livelihoods of fishermen.

- Gear regulation and seasonal bans in coastal and marine areas are recommended to ensure easy migration of *Hilsa* and *jatka* upstream. It is essential to formulate as well as implement marine *Hilsa* fishing policies and restrictive zoning in the Bangladeshi section of the Bay of Bengal.

- More *Hilsa* sanctuaries (in addition to the existing five) should be established both in riverine and marine ecosystems to maintain stock levels.

5.1.2 For India

- Need to strictly adhere to the mesh size (100 mm or 4 inch) regulation especially at estuary mouth to control exploitation of *Hilsa* of below 500 g brooders to facilitate them to breed at least once in the life cycle.

- During the peak spawning period (October-November) a ban on *Hilsa* fishing within a 10 km radius of identified breeding grounds should be enforced. During this period, designated riverine *Hilsa* fishers need to be adequately compensated by the Government towards maintenance of their livelihood.

- To conserve *Hilsa* fisheries, a stringent ban should be imposed on capturing of juveniles. Strict law enforcement is required to prevent the destruction of *Hilsa* fisheries. During March-May, most of the juveniles (80-150 mm) start downstream migration. In Bangladesh, there is a restriction on the use of bag and scoop nets for catching *Hilsa* below 230 mm. A similar policy in India during these months by banning bag nets, lift nets and small meshed gill nets (1 inch) would facilitate juveniles migration to the sea and assist in reaching the original stock levels.

- It is expected that most of the upstream migrating *Hilsa* will congregate near Farakka Barrage. Fishing may be prohibited within 5 km of the barrage round the year to protect the species and facilitate brooders for spawning in the area.

- Improvement of the aquatic habitat with more emphasis on wise water management measures in the estuary mouth may encourage more brooders to migrate upstream.

- Decline of catch per unit effort (CPUE) data *vis à vis* reduction of average size species depicts that stock of *Hilsa* in the Indian part of the Bay of Bengal appears to be closed to its sustainable exploitation limit and needs immediate efforts for stock assessment and management.

- Bottom trawling in shallow continental shelf (up to 30 km) should be strictly banned to save the shallow marine habitat

- A focused study in India concentrating on possible spawning grounds for *Hilsa*, submerged sand bars near and within the estuaries of Matla, Thakuran and Raimongal rivers should be explored. These grounds (especially during the breeding season)—after proper demarcation—may be declared 'protected area' for *Hilsa*.

- The West Bengal Fishing Act (1984) needs to be amended appropriately to consider the aspect of pollution.

5.1.3 Common for the Regional Ecosystem

- The ban on *Hilsa* fishing to protect the juvenile and brood fish should be imposed in both Bangladesh and India at the same time.

- *Hilsa* migration depends on water flow and depth. To maintain proper water flow, appropriate measures are needed at Padma-Meghna and Hooghly-Bhagirathi river systems.

- To ensure conservation of *Hilsa* and other fish species, a complete ban on use and manufacture of zero-meshed nets is required.
- Establishment of any polluting industry and power station in the estuary or close to the spawning grounds is not advisable for the health of the estuarine fishery and the mangrove ecosystems.
- It is time that we take up a thorough stock assessment of marine and freshwater *Hilsa* at regular intervals using a common methodology for Bangladesh and India.
- The study observes the necessity to maintain an environmental flow of freshwater in estuaries and associated mangrove ecosystems for sustainable *Hilsa* fishery.
- Opening of *Hilsa* corridor by removing barriers of bag nets and other small meshed nets from the estuary mouths two days before and after the full moon and new moon of every month.
- There should be research on market dynamics and its effect on *Hilsa* conservation.
- Community-driven approach in mass awareness building on conservation of *Hilsa* is necessary to provide alternative livelihood support.
- Joint initiatives must be taken in technology transfer for captive breeding and domestication of *Hilsa*.

5.1.4 *Reflections on Future Research*

- Some future research areas, both short and long term, have been identified by the JRT.
- Investigation on water quality and pollution and its effect on sustainable *Hilsa* fishery.
- Climate change impact on spawning and migration patterns of *Hilsa*.
- Determination of ecological flow in the rivers and estuaries to ensure spawning and migration of *Hilsa*.
- Exploring possibilities of creation and maintenance of fish ladder/ passes for *Hilsa*.
- Identification of new spawning grounds of *Hilsa* in India and Bangladesh for conservation.
- Investigation on stakeholders perceptions for formulation of better conservation strategies.
- Long-term length frequency analysis to work out mean sustainable yield (MSY), standing stock, recruitment, mortality rate and overall health of the population along with other biological observations in the transboundary Ganga-Brahmaputra river system and northern Bay of Bengal.

References

Abdurahiman, K.P., T. Harishnayak, P.U Zacharia and K.S. Mohamed (2004). "Length-weight Relationship of Commercially Important Marine Fshes and Shellfishes of the Southern Coast of Karnataka, India", *NAGA, World Fish Center Quarterly* 27(1 and 2).

Ali, M.Y. (1991). *Towards Sustainable Development: Fisheries Resources of Bangladesh*. Dhaka: IUCN.

Al-Nasiri, S.A. and M.A. Al-Mukhtar (1988). "On the Biology of Sbour, *Hilsa ilisha* (Hamilton) (Pisces, Clupeidae) from Ashar Canal, Basrah", *Pakistan Journal of Zoology* 20: 321-28.

Ambily, V. and S.B. Nandan (2010). "Length-weight Relationship, Relative Condition Factor (Kn) and Morphometry of *Arius subrostratus* (Valenciennes, 1840) from a Coastal Wetland in Kerala", *Indian J. Fish.* 57(4): 39-44.

Anon (1957 to 2003). *Annual Reports*. Barrackpore: Central Inland Fisheries Research Institute.

———. (2000-2011). Reports of Department of Fisheries. Government of West Bengal.

APHA (1995). *Standard Methods for the Examination of Water and Wastewater.* 19th ed. New York: American Public Health Association.

Beyer, J.E. (1987). "On Length–Weight Relationships: Part 1—Computing the Mean Weight of the Fish of a Given Length Class", *Fishbyte* 5: 11-13.

Bhanot, K.K. (1973). "Observation on the Spawning of *Hilsa ilisha* (Hamilton) in the Hooghly Estuary", *Journal of Inland Fisheries Society of India* 5: 50-54.

Bhaumik, Utpal (2010). *Status of Fishery of Indian Shad (Tenualosa illisha) with reference to the Hooghly River System.* 21st All India Congress of Zoology. December 21-23. pp.66-81.

Bhaumik, Utpal and A.P. Sharma (2011a). "The Fishery of Indian Shad (*Tenualosa ilisha*) in the Bhagirathi-Hooghly River System", Fishing Chimes, 31 (8): 21-27.

Bhaumik, Utpal, Malay Naskar and A.P. Sharma (2011b). "Size Distribution, Length-Weight Relationship and Sex Ratio of the Hilsa (*Tenualosa ilisha*) in the Hooghly Estuarine System", *J. Inland Fish. Soc. India* 43(2): 1-5.

Bhaumik, Utpal, N.P. Srivastava, B.B Satpathy, M.K. Mukhopadhyay and A.P. Sharma (2011c). "Impact of Hydro-ecology on Fish Migration in Selected East Coast Estuaries", *J. Inland Fish.Soc.India* 43(1): 1-9.

Bhaumik, Utpal and A.P. Sharma (2012). Present Status of hilsa in Hooghly-Bhagirathi river, *CIFRI Bulletin* 179: 42p.

Chacko, P.I. and B. Krishnamurthy (1948). *A Preliminary Note on the Hilsa Fishery Investigations in South India.* Proc. 35th Indian Science Congress, Pt. III. p.204.

Chandra, R. (1994). *Some Endangered, Vulnerable and Rare Miscellaneous Fishes of Ganga River System: Hilsa ilisha (Ham.) and Setipinna phasa (Ham.)*. Paper presented in the National Seminar on Endangered Fishes of India. April. Barrackpore: Central Inland Capture Fisheries Research Institute. pp.7-11

Chandra, R., K.R. Srivastava and R.K. Saxena (1987). *Effect of Farakka Barrage on the Spawning and Fishery of Indian Shad, Hilsa ilisha (Ham.).* Symposium on the Impact of Current Land Use Pattern and Water Resources Development on Riverine Fisheries. April 25-27. Barrackpore: Central Inland Capture Fisheries Research Institute. p.67.

Clark, N. (1934). "Maturity of the California Sardine *(Sardina caerulea)* Determined by Ova Diameter Measurements", *Calif. Fish. Bull.* 42: 49.

Day, F. (1878). *The Fishes of India: Being a Natural History of the Fishes Known to Inhabit the Seas and Fresh Waters of India, Burma, and Ceylon.* Part 4. London: W.M. Dawson and Sons.

De, D.K. and N.C. Dutta (1990). "Studies on Certain Aspects of the Morphology of Indian Shad Hilsa", *Indian Journal of Fisheries* 37 (3): 189-98.

De, D.K. (1986). *Studies on the Food and Feeding Habit of Hilsa, Hilsa ilisha (Hamilton) of the Hooghly Estuarine System and Some Aspects of its Biology.* Ph.D. Thesis. Calcutta University. p.285.

———. (2001). *Proceedings of the International Terubok (Tenualosa Sp.) Conference.* September 11-12. Sarawak, Malaysia. pp.25-51.

De, D.K. and B.N. Saigal (1989). "Spawning of *Hilsa, Tenualosa ilisha* in Hooghly Estuary", *J. Inland Fish. Soc. India* 21: 46-48.

DoF (2008). *Fisheries Statistical Yearbook of Bangladesh* 2006-07. Bangladesh: Department of Fisheries, MoFL.

———. (2011). *Fisheries Statistical Yearbook of Bangladesh* 2009-10. Bangladesh: Department of Fisheries, MoFL.

Dubey, G.P. (1994). "Endangered, Vulnerable and Rare Fishes of West Coast River System of India", Paper presented in the National Seminar on *Endangered Fishes of India.* April. Barrackpore: Central Inland Capture Fisheries Research Institute. pp.77-95

Ecoutin, J.M., J.J. Albaret and S. Trape (2005). "Length–Weight Relationships for Fsh Populations of a Relatively Undisturbed Tropical Estuary: The Gambia", *Fisheries Research* 72, 347–51.

Fischer W. and G. Bianchi (1984). FAO *Species Identification Sheet for Fishery Purposes.* Western Indian Ocean (Fishing Area 51), Vol. I. Rome: FAO.

Fish Base (2004). *FishBase.* World Wide Web electronic database. Retrieved in September 2004 from *http://www.fishbase.org.*

Ghosh, A.K. (1987). "Effects of Environmental Modifications on Riverine Fishes of India", Paper presented in the Symposium on the *Impact of Current Land Use Pattern and Water Resources Development on Riverine Fisheries.* April. Barrackpore: Central Inland Capture Fisheries Research Institute.

Gopalakrishnan, V. (1969). "Observations on the Present Status of *Hilsa* Fisheries in the Hooghly-Matlah Estuarine System (West Bengal, India)", *Proc. Indian Science Congress* 56(3): 539-40.

Haldar, G.C. and M.A. Rahman (1998). "Ecology of *Hilsa, Tenualosa ilisha* (Hamilton)", in Mazid, M.A. and S.J.M. Blaber, *Hilsa Fisheries Research in Bangladesh*. Proceedings of the Workshop on Hilsa Research. March 3-4. Dhaka, Bangladesh. pp.11-19

Halder, G.C. (2004). *Present Status of the Hilsa Fishery in Bangladesh*. Completion report of studies conducted under the ARDMCS, GEF component and FFP. Report No. 38.8. Dhaka, Bangladesh: Department of Fisheries.

Haroon, Y. (1998). "*Hilsa* shad: Fish for the Teeming Millions, New Management Alternatives Needed for the *Hilsa* Young", *Shad Journal* 3: 7.

Harrison, T.D. (2001). "Length-Weight Relationships of Fishes from South African Estuaries", *J. Appl. Ichthyol.* 17: 46-48.

Hora, S.L. (1938). "A Preliminary Note on the Spawning Grounds and Bionomics of the So-called Indian Shad, *Hilsa Ilisha* (Ham.) in the River Ganges", *Records of Indian Museum* 40: 147-58.

———. (1941). "Life History and Wanderings of Hilsa in West Bengal Waters", *Journal of Asiatic Society (Sci)* 6 (2): 93-112.

Hora, S.L. and K.K. Nair (1940). "Further Observations on the Bionomics and Fishery of the Indian Shad, *Tenualosa ilisha* (Hamilton) in Bengal Waters", *Records of the Indian Museum* 42(1): 35-50.

———. (1940a). "Further Observation Bionomics and Fishery of Indian Shad , *Hilsa Ilisha* in Bengal Waters", *Records of Indian Museum* 42: 35-50.

———. (1940a). "The Jatka Fish of Eastern Bengal and its Significance in the Fishery of the so-called Indian Shad, *Hilsa Ilisha* (Ham.)", *Records of the Indian Museum* 42, 553-65.

Hossain, M.M. (1985). "Spawning Times and Early Life History of *Hilsa ilisha* in Bangladesh Waters". Unpublished M.S. thesis. Canada: University of British Columbia. p.90.

Iquabal, Farhed. Kazi. and A.R.A. Taha (2009). *Floods of Bangladesh: Influenced by Climate Change and Variability*. Dhaka: Bangladesh Nature Conservation Society.

Jhingran, A.G. and R.A. Gupta (1987). "Status, Dynamics and Exploitation of Indian Shad, *Hilsa Ilisha* (Hamilton) of the Ganga", Paper presented in the Symposium on the *Impact of Current Land Use Pattern and Water Resources Development on Riverine Fisheries*. April. Barrackpore: Central Inland Capture Fisheries Research Institute.

Jhingran, V. G. and A.V. Natarajan (1973). "Fishery Resources of the Chilka Lake and its Bearing on Fisheries in Adjacent Areas of Bay of Bengal", Proceedings of Symposium *Living Resources of the Seas around India*. Special. Pub. CMFRI. pp.365-72.

Jones, S. (1954). "*Hilsa* Investigation at the Central Inland Fisheries Research Station: Aims and Achievements", *J. As/at. Soc. (Sci.)* 20(1): 65-67.

———. (1959a). "Fishing Methods for the Indian Shad, *Hilsa ilisha* (Hamilton) in the Indian Region: Part 1", *J. Bombay Nat. H/st. Soc.* 56(2): 250-75.

———. (1959b). "Fishing Methods for the Indian Shad, *Hilsa ilisha* (Hamilton) in the Indian Region: Part 2", *J. Bombay Nat. H/st. Soc.* 56(3): 423-48.

Jones, S. and P.M.G. Menon (1951). "Observations on the Life History of the Indian Shad, *Hilsa ilisha* (Ham.)", *Proc. Indian. Acad. Sci.* 31(3): 101-25.

Kalayci, F., N. Samsun, S. Bilgin and O. Samsun (2007). "Length-Weight Relationship of 10 Fish Species Caught by Bottom Trawl and Mid-water Trawl from the Middle Black Sea, Turkey", *Turkish Journal of Fisheries and Aquatic Sciences* 7: 33-36.

Kowtal, G.V. (1994). "Endangered, Vulnerable and Rare Food Fishes of the East Coast River System", Paper presented in the National Seminar on *Endangered Fishes of India*. April. Barrackpore: Central Inland Capture Fisheries Research Institute. pp.57-61

Master Plan Organization (MPO) (1986). *National Master Plan, Final Report*. Volume 1. Dhaka

Mathur, P.K. (1964). "Studies on the Maturity and Fecundity of the *Hilsa, Hilsa iisha* (Hamilton) in the Upper Stretches of Ganga", *Indian J. Fish.* 11(1): 423-48.

Mazid, M.A. and S. Islam (1991). *Hilsa Fishery Developement and Management: A Report* (in Bengali). Mymensingh, Bangladesh: Fisheries Research Institute. p.16.

Morato, T., P. Afonso, P. Loirinho, J.P. Barreiros, R.S. Sanstos and R.D.M. Nash (2001). "Length-Weight Relationships for 21 Costal Fish Species of the Azores, North-eastern Atlantic", *Fisheries Research* 50: 297-302.

Momi, M.A. (2007). *The Potential of the Artisanal Hilsa in Bangladesh: An Economically Efficient Fishery*. Iceland: United Nations University.

Mukhopadhyay, M.K. (1994). "Some Threatened Estuarine Fishes of India", Paper presented in the *National Seminar on Endangered Fishes of India*. Barrackpore: Central Inland Capture Fisheries Research Institute. pp.229-35

Muto, E.Y., L.S.H. Soares and C.L.D.B. Rossi-Wongtschowski (2000). "Length-Weight Relationship of Marine Fish Species off São Sebastião System, São Paulo, Southeastern Brazil", *Naga, The ICLARM Quarterly* 23(4).

Naidu, M.R. (1939). *Report on Survey of the Fisheries of Bengal, Calcutta.*

Pillay, S.R. and H. Rosa (1963). "Synopsis of Biological Data on *Hilsa, Hilsa Ilisha* (Ham.) 1822. *FAO Fisheries Synopsis* 25: 61.

Pillay, T.V.R. (1955). "The Biology and Fisheries of the *Hilsa, Ilisha (Hamilton)*: A Review", *Proc. Indo-Pacific. Fish. Coun.* 6(2): 211 -19.

———. (1958). "Biology of the *Hilsa, Hilsa ilisha* (Hamilton) of the River Hooghly"", *Indian J. Fish.* 5: 201-57.

Pisolkav, M.D. (1994). Declined fish species of Tapti River and its tributaries. Paper presented in the National Seminar on Endangered Fishes of India (109-116 pp). Barrackpore: Central Inland Capture Fisheries Research Institute.

Quddus, M.M.A. and M. Shafi (1983). *The Fish Resources of the Bay of Bengal* (In Bengali). Dhaka: Bangla Academy. p.476.

Qureshi, M.R. (1968). "Problem Concerning Fishery of *Hilsa ilisha* in the River Indus"", *Pakistan J. Sci. Ind. Res.* 11: 85-94.

Rahman, A.K.A. (1989). *Freshwater Fishes of Bangladesh*. Dhaka: Zoological Soc. Bangladesh.

———. (2005). *Freshwater Fishes of Bangladesh*. 2nd edn. Dhaka: Zoological Soc. Bangladesh. p.394.

Rahman, M.A., M.A. Alam, T. Ahmed, Flura, S.J. Hasan, K.K.U. Ahmed and M. Zaher (2012). *Hilsha Fisheries Research and Management* (In Bengali). Extension Man. 42. Bangladesh Fisheries Research Institute. p.32.

Rahman, M.A., M.A. Alam, S.J. Hasan and M. Zaher (2012). Hilsa (*Tenualosa ilisha* Ham.) "Fishery Management in Bangladesh", in *Hilsa: Status of Fishery and Potential for Aquaculture*, The World Fish Centre, Dhaka: 40-60.

Rahman, M.J. (2001). "Population Biology and Management of the *Hilsa* Shad (*Tenualosa ilisha*) in Bangladesh". Ph.D. Thesis. England: The University of Hull.

Rahman, M.J. and I.G. Cowx (2006). "Lunar Periodicity in Growth Increment Formation in Otoliths of *Hilsa* shad (*Tenualosa ilisha*, Clupeidae) in Bangladesh Waters", *Fisheries Research* 81: 342-344.

Raja, B.T.A. (1985). A review of the biology and fisheries of *Hilsa* in the upper Bay of Bengal. Marine Fishery Resource Management in the Bay of Bengal. BOBP/WP/37:66.

Rajyalakshmi, T. (1973). "The Population Characteristics of the Godavari *Hilsa* over the Years 1963-67", *Indian J. Fish.* 20 (1): 78-94.

Ramakrishnaiah, M. (1972). *Biology of Hilsa ilisha (Hamilton) from the Chilka Lake with an Account on its Racial Status* 19(1 & 2).

Reuben, S., S.S. Dan, M.V. Somaraju, V. Philipose and T.V. Sathianandan (1992). "The Resources of *Hilsa* shad, *Hilsa* ilisha (Hamilton), along the Northeast Coast of India", *Indian Journal of Fisheries* 39 (3.4): 169-81.

Shafi, M. and M.M.A. Quddus (1982). *Fisheries of Bangladesh* (In Bengali). Dhaka: Bangla Academy. p.444.

Southwell, T. and B. Prashad (1918). "On *Hilsa* Investigations in Bengal, Bihar and Orissa", *Bull. Dept. Fish. Bengal, Bihar and Orissa* 11: 1-12.

Strum, L.M.G. (1978). "Aspects of the Biology of *Scombemorus maculates* (Mitchill) in Trinidad", *Journal of Fish Biology* 13: 155-72.

Volvich, L. and S. Appelbaum (2001). "Length to Weight Relationship of Sea Bass *Lates calcarifer* (Bloch) Reared in a Closed Recirculating System", *The Israeli Journal of Aquaculture–Bamidgeh* 53(3-4): 158-63.

Appendices: Photographic Representation of Some Activities During the Study in Bangladesh

(Photographs by Dr M. Niamul Naser)

Gill nets are commonly used for *Hilsa* fishing in Mehgna river; lamp floats (right) are used at night fishing.

Ice preserved *Hilsa* were transported to the wholesale market at Chandpur; packing facilities at Chandpur wholesale market (right).

Fishermen are preparing for *Hilsa* fishing at Bhola; unique scoop-net *Hilsa* fishing at Paba, Rajshahi.

Commonly fished *jatka* at lower Meghna river basin; officials are in action during banned period.